Communities of the Soul

McGill-Queen's Studies in the History of Religion

Volumes in this series have been supported by the Jackman Foundation of Toronto.

Communities
of the Soul

A Short History of Religion in Puerto Rico

~

JOSÉ E. IGARTUA

McGill-Queen's University Press

Montreal & Kingston • London • Chicago

© McGill-Queen's University Press 2021

ISBN 978-0-2280-0839-2 (cloth)
ISBN 978-0-2280-0840-8 (paper)
ISBN 978-0-2280-0959-7 (ePDF)
ISBN 978-0-2280-0960-3 (ePUB)

Legal deposit fourth quarter 2021
Bibliothèque nationale du Québec

Printed in Canada on acid-free paper that is 100% ancient forest
free (100% post-consumer recycled), processed chlorine free

We acknowledge the support of the Canada Council for the Arts.

Nous remercions le Conseil des arts du Canada de son soutien.

Library and Archives Canada Cataloguing in Publication

Title: Communities of the soul : a short history of religion in
    Puerto Rico / José E. Igartua.
Names: Igartua, José E., 1946- author.
Series: McGill-Queen's studies in the history of religion. Series
    two ; 90.
Description: Series statement: McGill-Queen's studies in the
    history of religion. Series two ; 90 | Includes bibliographical
    references and index.
Identifiers: Canadiana (print) 20210294329 | Canadiana (ebook)
    20210294493 | ISBN 9780228008392 (cloth) | ISBN 9780228008408
    (paper) | ISBN 9780228009597 (ePDF) | ISBN 9780228009603
    (ePUB)
Subjects: LCSH: Puerto Rico—Religion. | LCSH: Puerto Rico—
    Religious life and customs.
Classification: LCC BL2566.P9 I33 2021 | DDC 200.97295—dc23

Contents

~

Figures

~

Preface

Religion is a fundamental component of Puerto Rican society. A 2014 Pew Research Center survey reported that 99 per cent of Puerto Ricans believed in God, 86 per cent believed in hell, 76 per cent said religion was very important in their lives, and nearly half attended religious services at least once a week; only 10 per cent declared themselves neither Catholic nor Protestant.[1] From the cosmology of the Taíno to the wide array of Judaeo-Christian churches, synagogues, and sects and the syncretic religious worldviews of the practitioners of spiritism, *santería*, *brujería*, and the customers of the *botánicas*, religious practice in its many forms still permeates the lives of a large majority of present-day Puerto Ricans.

But why is this of interest to me? I can claim to be Puerto Rican, having been born in Aguadilla, on the north-west tip of the island, to a Puerto Rican father and a French-Canadian mother. But I lived there only the first four months of my life, after which the family moved to Quebec, where I was raised by my mother, my father moving back to Puerto Rico when I was a pre-schooler. I first revisited Puerto Rico in 1979 to reconnect with my father and meet his side of the family. I am a historian,[2] so I learned a little of the island's history during that visit. I was struck by the similarities in the political trajectories of Puerto Rico and Quebec. Both were societies twice colonized, once by a mother country that infused its colony with its culture, its history, and its religion, and a second time by a conquering imperial power of different language, religion, and cultural values.

I became interested in the history of religious practice in Puerto Rico by intellectual accident. After my retirement in 2008, I published a comparative overview of the history of Quebec and Puerto Rican nationalism in the *Revista de ciencias sociales* of the University of Puerto Rico in Río Piedras.[3] A colleague who read this article asked me about the similarities and differences in the Catholic church's involvement in politics in both places. My response was to start looking into the history of the Catholic church in Puerto Rico with a view to comparing it to that of the church in Quebec. At the outset, the most visible difference I noted was the growing importance of Protestantism, particularly Pentecostalism, in twentieth-century Puerto Rico, which had no equivalent in Quebec. As I read about popular religious practices, about the Catholic church's precarious situation in Puerto Rico, and about the many other forms of religious practices on the island, the idea for this book took shape.

Before we proceed, I must spell out what I understand by "religion" and "religious practices." There is no accepted definition of religion,[4] and this is not the place for an extended debate. I take religion to be a collective set of beliefs about the supernatural origins of the world and about rules of conduct within human groups that allow for their cohesion and survival, based on belief in life in the hereafter. I consider this definition broad enough to encompass at once the Taíno worldview and those held by Freemasons and Unitarians as well as Catholics, Protestants, Jews, and Muslims, all of whom are present in contemporary Puerto Rico.

Long before print capitalism constituted nations as imagined communities,[5] religion provided real communities of the soul. Besides individual belief and faith, religion also encompasses individual and collective practices, which may be prescribed and regulated by organizations such as clergy or parochial assemblies, or more loosely by social rituals that serve to transmit knowledge of human, natural, or supernatural behaviour. In Puerto Rico, these practices range from formal ceremonies of baptism in various Christian denominations, which bring an individual into a community of believers, to commonplace vernacular expressions such as "¡*Ay bendito!*" ("Aw man," or "Oh my God") and the well-known celebrations of parishes' *fiestas patronales* (saints' feast days), which incorporate both religious and festive activities of sociability. From a sociological point of view, then, religion is an activity of community bonding and mutual help.

This is the first synthesis of the history of religion in Puerto Rico. Despite religion's age-old importance in Puerto Rican daily life, it hardly figures in the major textbooks on the island's history.[6] So I offer this book as an overview, based on the vast scholarly production on religious structures and practices in Puerto Rico. This production has come from historians, anthropologists, ethnographers, sociologists, and assorted other scholars from Puerto Rico and from elsewhere, written sometimes from a perspective critical of religion, sometimes in an apologetic vein. I try to avoid either position. As well, I try to see the subject within the larger context of Latin American religious history, with which it shares the features of a Catholic hierarchical structure, but with different forms of state interference in religious affairs. Protestantism's larger place on the island than most elsewhere in Latin America also sets it apart.[7]

Of necessity, I have not attempted archival research, although I rely on some printed primary sources. During my yearly winter stays in Puerto Rico since 2009, I have done library research in San Juan's academic institutions, conducted several interviews, and visited historical sites of popular religious ceremonies, including the shrines to Our Lady of Monserrate at Hormigueros and to the Virgen del Pozo at Sabana Grande, the Taíno ceremonial park at Caguana, near Utuado, and the Jacaná native archaeological site near Ponce (see figure o.1).

I have tried as much as possible to consider informal as well as formal forms of religious practices. Informal practices occur mainly within formal structures that encourage, allow, or restrict such practices. Because of the dearth of sources on religious practice before the nineteenth century, the first chapters deal more with structures than I would like, but the book tries to include as wide a variety of religious behaviour as possible.

Of necessity also, this short book offers generalizations about religious behaviour, but, as anthropologist Juan F. Caraballo Resto has reminded me,[8] members of each religious community vary in the extent of religious practice and in the roles of faith and social standing as reasons for belonging. Within Catholic communities, for instance, one can find the

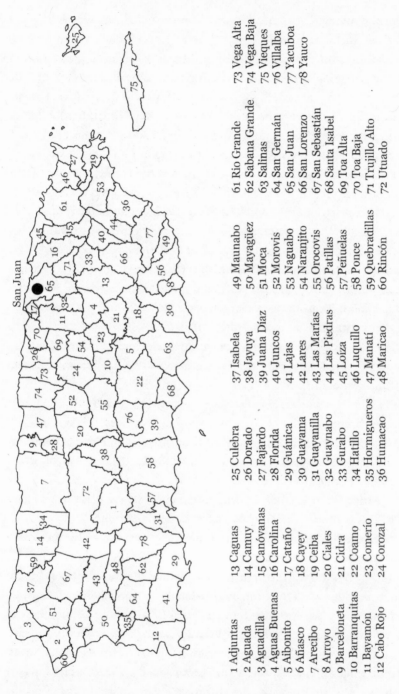

Figure 0.1 Puerto Rico municipalities.

San Juan

1 Adjuntas
2 Aguada
3 Aguadilla
4 Aguas Buenas
5 Aibonito
6 Añasco
7 Arecibo
8 Arroyo
9 Barceloneta
10 Barranquitas
11 Bayamón
12 Cabo Rojo

13 Caguas
14 Camuy
15 Canóvanas
16 Carolina
17 Cataño
18 Cayey
19 Ceiba
20 Ciales
21 Cidra
22 Coamo
23 Comerío
24 Corozal

25 Culebra
26 Dorado
27 Fajardo
28 Florida
29 Guánica
30 Guayama
31 Guayanilla
32 Guaynabo
33 Gurabo
34 Hatillo
35 Hormigueros
36 Humacao

37 Isabela
38 Jayuya
39 Juana Díaz
40 Juncos
41 Lajas
42 Lares
43 Las Marías
44 Las Piedras
45 Loíza
46 Luquillo
47 Manatí
48 Maricao

49 Maunabo
50 Mayagüez
51 Moca
52 Morovis
53 Naguabo
54 Naranjito
55 Orocovis
56 Patillas
57 Peñuelas
58 Ponce
59 Quebradillas
60 Rincón

61 Río Grande
62 Sabana Grande
63 Salinas
64 San Germán
65 San Juan
66 San Lorenzo
67 San Sebastián
68 Santa Isabel
69 Toa Alta
70 Toa Baja
71 Trujillo Alto
72 Utuado

73 Vega Alta
74 Vega Baja
75 Vieques
76 Villalba
77 Yacuboa
78 Yauco

profoundly devout as well as those who attend church because it is the norm in their social circles. In the Jewish and Muslim communities also, there are those who regularly attend the synagogue or the mosque, and those who strongly identify as Jews or Muslims but seldom take part in their community's religious rituals.

The book begins with the religious beliefs of the Taíno natives who populated the island when explorers from Spain set foot on it. It examines the Taíno creation myth, the depth of symbolic meanings in their cosmology, their binary concept of the world and society, physical manifestations of the spirit world, the role of religious and secular leaders, and the legacy of the Taíno worldview.

Chapter 2 offers an overview of the Catholic church in Spain from the sixteenth to the eighteenth centuries. Spain provided both the institutional structure of the church in Puerto Rico and its clerical manpower during that period. The chapter also outlines the popular religious practices that Spanish settlers would bring to Puerto Rico.

Chapter 3 sketches how the island's Catholic church established its institutions from the sixteenth to the eighteenth centuries, noting the small numbers and the uneven quality of its clergymen, the physical distance between priests and the laity in the interior of the island, and the laity's greater reliance on itself than on the institutional church to satisfy its spiritual needs.

Chapter 4 traces the extension of formal Catholicism on the island in the early nineteenth century and the imperial context, which pitted metropolitan Spain against the *criollos'* (native-born) desires for autonomy. The metropolis suspected *criollo* priests of disloyalty, so replaced most of them with Spaniards. This increased the social distance between clergy and laity and left room for the latter to continue the popular religious practices of its forebears.

During the last third of the nineteenth century, the Catholic church faced challenges that would weaken it before the island's conquest by the United States. Chapter 5 shows how the church's institutional foundations were shaken by changes to the church's status in Spain and by the poor quality of Spanish priests on the island. Spanish migrants to the island continued to bring with them metropolitan popular religious practices. This period witnessed the formation of the first Protestant congregations in Puerto Rico, as well as the increasing public presence of Freemasonry, spiritism, and its local folk variant, *espiritismo*, as forms of community-based belief systems.

Puerto Rico's Catholic church was further weakened by the US conquest of the island in 1898. Chapter 6 shows how the church lost its status as an institution of the state, its right to teach religion in public schools, and most of its Spanish-speaking clergymen, who were replaced principally by Americans, further distancing the church from its Puerto Rican flock, while the island's new administration favoured Protestantism. Catholicism continued to be challenged by spiritism, whose practitioners sometimes claimed to be Catholics as well. Local communities saw the emergence of female and male lay preachers who called for a rejuvenation of faith and religious behaviour, filling the spiritual void created by the church's faint presence.

Chapter 7 traces the institutional arrival of Protestantism on the island in the first half of the twentieth century, outlining the appeal of more community-based forms of religious structures. This was particularly true of Pentecostal communities from the 1930s onward, as they rested on an egalitarian relationship among members, personal involvement in the supernatural, and a strong sense of belonging, the price of which was exemplary behaviour that differentiated these groups from the broader island population.

Chapter 8 examines the Catholic church's travails in the second third of the twentieth century, as the church Americanized while Puerto Rican cultural nationalism began to rise. Popular Catholic religious practices persisted, mostly outside the purview of the church, which increasingly opposed the island's popular governor, Luis Muñoz Marín (in office 1949–65), and the Catholic political party failed dismally in the 1960s. The appearance of liberation theology challenged the church's ingrained conservatism, which ultimately prevailed.

Chapter 9 illustrates the growing diversity of religious practice today by describing the continuing appeal of evangelical Protestantism and the creation of Jewish and Muslim communities.

The last chapter returns to the theme of non-institutional forms of religious practice, exploring the persistence of popular Christianity and the various forms of faith healing in the late twentieth century.

As the Conclusion notes, the practice of religion in Puerto Rico will continue to evolve with the broad variety of communities of the soul that inhabit the island. It will remain a vital component of *puertorriqueñidad*.

The present synthesis is not as comprehensive as I would like. For instance, I am well aware of the sizable migration of Puerto Ricans to the US mainland since 1945 and of the frequent *vayven* (comings and goings) between the island and the mainland and of the resulting close family ties, but I have not attempted to inquire into the Puerto Rican communities of the soul on the US mainland and their interactions with the island, as their situation depended on their size, their age, their location, and their relations with other Spanish- and English-speaking communities. These contexts were different in New York, New Jersey, Connecticut, Massachusetts, Illinois, Pennsylvania, California, Florida, and elsewhere on the mainland, so generalizations would be a challenge. The fraught relations between Puerto Rican Catholics and the church hierarchy in New York City, for example, would be difficult to summarize.[9]

Another topic not discussed at any length below is Afro-Caribbean religious practices on the island. Before the arrival of Cuban immigrants in the 1960s, these cannot be documented, attests Rafael López Valdés, the authority on the history of African institutions in the Spanish Caribbean.[10] There are a few short mentions of such practices in official government and ecclesiastical documents, and I make brief reference to them. Dealing with the post-1960 links between practices of *santería* on the island and the mainland would have required inquiring further into the role of Cuban migrants to the island and to the mainland and their own *vayven*. I had decided at the outset of my research that I would focus on the island society, notwithstanding the importance of circular migration between the island and the US mainland.

I have found very little scholarly production on the history of "historical" Protestant denominations in the period after 1945, so this topic also lacks any treatment.

Despite these shortcomings, I hope the book gives readers an appetite for learning more about the history of religion on the island of Puerto Rico.

~

Acknowledgments

My colleague Fernande Roy, of the History Department at the Université du Québec à Montréal, was the person who inquired over ten years ago about the role of the Catholic church in Puerto Rican politics, after she had read my article comparing Quebec and Puerto Rico published in the *Revista de Ciencias Sociales*. Her question led to my broader investigation of the history of religion on the island. I would like to thank her again for her interest in my work.

I must express gratitude for the help I have received throughout this project. I want to thank first of all anthropologist Jorge Duany, now of Florida International University, who introduced me to Puerto Rican social-science scholarship when he was still at the Río Piedras campus of the University of Puerto Rico, and whose extensive 1998 review of scholarly production on popular religiosity on the island was a welcome starting point for much of my investigation. Professor Duany also put me in contact with sociologist Juan Manuel Carrión, with whom I shared an interest in nationalism, and who was kind enough to publish my comparative article on Quebec and Puerto Rico in the *Revista de Ciencias Sociales*. Professor Carrión also shared some observations on contemporary Puerto Rico. My gratitude as well to Professor Samuel Silva Gotay, whose scholarly work I have much relied on, and whose gracious company I was fortunate to enjoy. Professor Humberto García Muñiz, of the University of Puerto Rico's Institute of Caribbean Studies in Río Piedras, provided a welcoming environment and beneficial advice. My fellow historian and Aguadillana relative, Haydée E. Reichard de Cancio, PhD, who has written broadly on the theme of religion in Puerto Rican history, was generous with her research and advice on this project.

Several persons graciously gave me interviews about their communities or about their research into religious practice in Puerto Rico. For granting me interviews I wish to thank Diego Mendelbaum, spiritual leader of the conservative Shaare Zedek synagogue, Norman Patz, visiting rabbi at the Beth Shalom synagogue, Mendel Zarchi, rabbi at the Rohr Shabad-Lubovitch synagogue, Imam Ibrahim Abusalem, of the Islamic Center in Río Piedras, Imam Yunus Fasasi, of the Vega Alta mosque, Imam Nabil El Fallah of the Montehiedra mosque, the late Jesuit historian Fernando Picó, who shared with me his thoughts on the place of religion in the island's historiography, and anthropologist Juan F. Caraballo Resto, of the Cayey campus of the University of Puerto Rico and of the Protestant Theological Seminary in Río Piedras, who allowed me to benefit from his extensive and considered knowledge of Muslim communities.

I also want to thank the affable administration and staff of the libraries on the Río Piedras campus of the University of Puerto Rico for giving me access to their collections, and the interlibrary loan services at the Université du Québec à Montréal for their rapid answers to my requests. I also thank McGill University in Montreal, the Centro de estudios avanzados de Puerto Rico y el Caribe in Old San Juan, and the Seminario Evangélico de Puerto Rico in Río Piedras for the use of their libraries. To the anonymous members of various religious communities on the island, to the residents of Isla Verde who have listened to my musings about this project, to my Puerto Rican relatives, and to my immediate family, who have joined me for the research time I spent on the island, I want to express my profound gratitude. I also thank the two anonymous readers who assessed the manuscript for McGill-Queen's University Press: their insightful comments and their valuable suggestions improved the book. The guidance of my copy editor, John Parry, and of the editorial staff at the press helped shape the final product. The errors contained in this work remain, of course, solely my responsibility.

Communities of the Soul

1

Life and Religion among the Taíno

Each year, in November, the town of Jayuya, in the mountainous centre of the island, holds the National Indigenous Festival to celebrate its Taíno[1] roots. Among the festivities is a pageant featuring Taíno princesses, the woman and girl who most look Taíno in features and costumes. The fact that no one has any idea of what a Taíno costume looked like – it is supposed that the women wore only a loincloth – is of no consequence. Tradition is invented to suit contemporary needs.[2] There is a lot of room for invention, as little is known about the Taíno at the time of their encounter with Europeans in 1493. Within two decades Taíno society was dissolved by war and disease and left little besides place names, archaeological sites, artefacts, and mitochondrial DNA.[3] These are found on the island and throughout the Greater Antilles, which include Cuba and Hispaniola (Haiti and the Dominican Republic).

In Puerto Rico the major sites of Taíno archaeology are the Taíno Ceremonial Center in Caguana, near Utuado in central Puerto Rico, and the Tibes Indigenous Ceremonial Center just north of Ponce on the south side of the island, an archaeological site displaying layers that reflect successive Indigenous populations since about the time of Christ and first occupied by the Taíno about 1000 AD.[4]

comes from European views

The main ethnographical sources on native religion date from the first contacts between Spaniards and Taíno. Thy are the notes made by the Catalan friar Ramón Pané, who accompanied Christopher Columbus on his second expedition to America (1493–96), and who was charged with living among the Taíno and learning their language, which he did from 1493 to 1498, but not living in a Taíno territory.[5] Pané has been called the first ethnographer. His original notes, written probably in a Catalan-affected Spanish, have not survived; what remains is an Italian translation included in a history of Christopher Columbus in 1676 by his son Fernando, and this translation has been translated back into Spanish, then into English and French.

It is from these archaeological and ethnographic sources, then, that scholars have attempted to draw sketches of Taíno society, culture, and religion. Both types of sources are of course contentious, and at times suspect. The archaeological record is often interpreted as having religious signification, particularly when there is no obvious secular explanation for the artefacts. But a distinction between the sacred and the secular would be foreign to the Taíno. As for Pané's notes, we should read them with Pané's medieval Catholic worldview and intended audience in mind; he casts them in the "compare and contrast" mode vis-à-vis his own culture, in order to make himself understood by his readers, notably the Spanish monarchs. The evidence is malleable and is often read in different ways by different scholars. I have relied on the interpretations that seem the most convincing to me. For instance, the archaeological reading of the petroglyphs at the Caguana Ceremonial Court suggests that Pané's understanding of religious petroglyphs is "applicable in this case."[6]

One of the functions of religion is to provide an understanding of the world and of one's place in it. Religions thus have creation myths, stories that account for the origins of the physical world, of humans – meaning the community that holds the creation myth – and the supernatural. A literal reading of the Bible, for instance, accounts for the creation of the world by God in six days. But it does not explain how God himself (or herself) came to be. Even contemporary science, in the form of the big bang theory, has no explanation for what was before the big bang, or indeed if time existed before it. It is not unusual for creation myths not to have logical coherence in their literal meanings. They are metaphorical stories. This was the case for the Taíno.

A SINGLE COSMOLOGY

Taíno religion was intimately linked to the Taíno's view of the world. Like other native societies in the Americas, the Taíno considered all of nature to be endowed with human-like features.[7] Everything – humans, rocks, trees, the sea, animals, even the weather – could possess a soul. The term "animism" (from the Latin *anima*, or soul) has been used to characterize this worldview. These souls have characteristics of personhood, characteristics that could be divided and shared through "social relations and interactions with other human and nonhuman beings, animals, spiritual and physical things, even landscapes."[8] Souls therefore could communicate with and influence one another, connected "by elaborate manipulation of symbols," as a noted scholar of Taíno religion, Antonio M. Stevens Arroyo, has shown.[9]

The Origins of the World

Unlike the creation stories told by the Bible or the big bang theory, Taíno stories imply an already-existing world. It is unclear whether the Taíno could not conceive of the world not existing or whether Pané did not "push" his respondents further on the issue, since he himself believed that God existed from all eternity. Stevens Arroyo suggests that "Taíno social perception was accomplished without historical consciousness."[10]

In Taíno mythology the world was created by the transformation of familiar entities. Its account of creation tells of a man named Yaya – translated as "Supreme Spirit" – who had a son, Yayael, whom he killed because the son wanted to slay the father. Yaya put his son's bones in a gourd, which he hung from the roof of his house. One day the father wanted to see his son and asked his wife to take down the gourd and open it. When the gourd opened, "many fish, large and small, emerged from it. Whereby, seeing that those bones had been changed into fish, they resolved to eat them." Later the same gourd, being dropped to the ground, produced the oceans as well as more fish.[11]

This story, as anthropologists have pointed out, tells many things at once: the importance of the oceans and rivers as a source of food; the gourd, as "uterine symbol, where the bones (as a seminal force) mixed with the 'amniotic' fluid gestated life; upon overturning the calabash, the amniotic fluid gushed out with fish, thus populating the oceans and rivers." But it also lays down some cultural rules, suggests archaeologist José R. Oliver: "(1) that sons, competitors of the chief/father, have to leave the natal home and establish their own house; and (2) that upon death, selected bones of the deceased will be consumed by the surviving relatives as a proper or ideal funerary ritual."[12] So Taíno myths can and should be read at many levels to fully understand them.

This mechanism of transformation of objects underlying the Yaya story also applied to humans. In another part of the creation myth, a man named Mácacoel was entrusted with watching over the primaeval cave in which the Taíno lived, so that he would see "where he would send or distribute the people." Mácacoel failed to return to the cave before sunrise as he was supposed to and was seized by the sun and turned into a stone. The sun captured others and changed them into trees.[13] As for the sun and the moon, they also came from "from a cave located in the country of a *cacique* [chief] named Mautiatihuel," whose name could be translated as "Lord of the Region of the Dawn."[14]

A *Binary World*

The Taíno view of the world is more interesting than its view of creation. For the Taíno, the world was made of opposites that had to be reconciled. Day and night, sun and moon, man and woman, natural and supernatural, rain and drought, land and sea, but also "appearance and illusion, the conscious and the unconscious, the lawful and the lawless, the regulated and the spontaneous, the expected and the unpredictable ... each was defined by its opposite. Reality consisted in reconciling the two."[15]

This binary reality could be acted upon by the *cemí* represented in various artefacts, including the petroglyphs that have survived in Taíno ceremonial centres and elsewhere. José R. Oliver defines the cemí not as an object but as a "numinous power, a driving or vital force that compels action; it is the power to cause, to effect, and also denotes a condition or state of being."[16] For example, the Taíno accounted for the creation of wooden cemís by trees moving their roots and calling for a *behique*, or shaman, to fashion a cemí from the wood of the tree.[17] Cemís could have good or evil effects and could be treated as living beings. Pané tells the following story:

Figure 1.1 Taíno *cemí* petroglyphs, Caguana, January 2012.

[The Taíno said] the zemi [cemí] they called Vaybrama ... had been burned in a war they had waged, and when they washed him with the juice of the root we said above was called yuca [cassava], from which they made cassava bread, he grew arms, and his eyes reappeared, and his body grew; and because yuca or the aforesaid root was very small in those days, after they washed him with yuca water, it was henceforth, as it now is, fat and very large. This zemi brought diseases to men, according to their belief, for which they sought the help of the priests or behiques, who were their prophets and theologians as has been said; these priests would respond that the disease had befallen them because they had been negligent or forgetful in bringing cassava bread and yams and other things to eat to the ministers who swept and cleaned the house or hermitage of Vaybrama, good zemi, and that he had told him so.[18]

The story is telling on many levels besides the curative powers of the yuca plant, which was central to Taíno diet. The dualism of the Taíno world is readily apparent. The Vaybrama cemí was evil, but needed protection; but it could also be a "good zemi" if cared for properly by its "ministers" – their self-serving purpose obvious in their explanation of disease. The yuca became "fat and very large" after having treated the Vaybrama cemí, which attests to this cemí's power. This cemí has been identified on the Jacaná site, near the Tibes site, north of Ponce.[19]

The Taíno's binary view of nature has been emphasized at length by Stevens Arroyo in *Cave of the Jagua*.[20] He has distributed the various Taíno cemís into two four-by-four tables, the first one with rows for the masculine and "twins generated from the masculine," and a parallel one with rows for the feminine and "twins generated from the feminine." The columns represent the "Order of Fruitfulness" and the "Order of Inversion." The spirits of fruitfulness "bring plant and food life, provide water for drinking and irrigation, and insure family fertility. On the other side are the unpredictable spirits who destroy this order. Death, sexual promiscuity, the intrusion of dead spirits into the affairs of the living, and the terrible hurricanes are powerful manifestations of numinous power. But unlike the Spirits of Fruitfulness, the unpredictable spirits serve to invert rather than to establish what is ordinary."[21] So, as examples of this binary classification, the male Lord of the yuca plant, Yucahu, represents fruitful strength, and his feminine counterpart, Attabeira, embodies the fertilizing powers of water; the feminine opposite of Attabeira is Guabancex, the power of the wind and of the hurricane, or the "untamed" and "indomitable" in the feminine nature, while the masculine in the Order of Inversion represents death.[22]

Cemís and Sacred Grounds

The archaeological evidence found at the Jacaná site, one of many Taíno sacred grounds in Puerto Rico, and its layout as well as its contents are congruent with what textual evidence of Taíno celebrations tells us. Archaeologist José R. Oliver notes the "structural correspondence" between the cemís on Hispaniola (present-day Haiti and the Dominican Republic) described by Fra Ramón Pané, and those that may be observed today at Caguana, so that he "reads" the Puerto Rican cemís from their description in Pané's text.[23] Cemís were at the centre of Taíno religious experience. They could be found in private homes and in the homes of the shamans, but the most visible collections of cemís are on the sacred grounds such as Jacaná and Tibes, and Caguana. Games and religious ceremonies were held on these sites' "ball courts"; their edges are often delimited by rows of boulders, some of which represent cemís. For instance, in Caguana one may observe various representations of female fertility figures[24] (see figure 1.1).

Taíno society, like other American native societies, or our own contemporary society for that matter, lived a life imbued with symbolism. The structure of Taíno families required balance of gender and age. Like their gods, members of a Taíno family had opposite but complementary roles. The attribution of tasks within a family was gendered: "It was men who cleared the fields and women who tended the gardens; and it was women who made the nets and men who used them to capture fishes."[25] This implies that the care of children rested with women and thus constrained their work-related mobility. The assignment of work tasks embodied the Taíno's binary view of the world: their gods, like them, were gendered and had gender-specific roles in the Taíno cosmology.

Children, too, had symbolic meaning. They represented life and continuity, and the family's bonds with both past – their parents' lineage – and the future, through their eventual spouses. Children were a gift from their gods: cemís could bring "good fortune in childbirth." But children were excluded from the shamanic ceremonies to cure the ill, so that they would not disturb the proceedings.[26]

BEHIQUES AND CACIQUES

Taíno society had two intertwined structures of social power and control. On the religious level, the *behique*, or shaman, was the intermediary between the Taíno and the supernatural, embodied in nature and in cemís. Since everyday life was conceived as the interaction between natural and supernatural, any malfunction, such as disease – physical or spiritual – could be addressed by invoking the supernatural. This was the role of the behique. Pané recounts the curing ceremonies performed by the behiques, whom he called "physicians." Before entering the house of the ill, the behique rubbed his face with black soot "so as to make the sick man believe whatever they wish about his illness." The behique hid a small amount of stones, bones, or meat in his mouth, then entered the ill person's house, chewed on some herbs to induce vomiting, chanted, then pulled on the patient's leg or sucked on his body to remove the evil, then blew the evil out of the house and spat out what he had in his mouth, explaining that a cemí had put it inside the ill person "because you did not pray to him or you did not build him some temple, or you did not give him some land." The behique's cure did not always work. When it failed, the dead patient's relatives had a ritual to find out from the dead whether the behique was responsible for the death; if the dead person considered the behique guilty, then the family gave the behique a beating, which, like the healing ceremony itself, was a symbolic ritual.[27]

On the political and military level, it was the cacique, or chief, who led Taíno society. He ruled by "charisma and entrepreneurship" and by his ability to convince his people to follow the course of action he advocated.[28] This involved ritualistic practices similar to those of the behique. In council meetings where decisions were taken, the cacique would snuff *cohoba*, a powder ground from the hallucinogenic seeds of the *cohóbana* tree, entering into a trance that connected him with the cemís in order to see into the future.[29] Like the behiques, the caciques were entrusted with the safekeeping of the cemís, which gave them power.

THE END OF THE TAÍNO?

As we saw above, Taíno society disintegrated within thirty years of the arrival of the Spaniards in Puerto Rico in 1493. Smallpox, famine, war, and forced labour accounted for the "precipitous" decline, from between 30,000 and 60,000 at contact. By the time of the first census in 1530, fewer than 1,200 natives were counted, most of them captured on other islands and brought over as slaves.[30] Some Taíno had fled to neighbouring islands, then returned and settled in the hills of Añasco and San Germán, in the west, where, according to the eighteenth-century chronicler Iñigo Abbad y Lasierra, a Benedictine monk, they began to intermingle with the descendants of Spaniards and Africans on the island only in the early eighteenth century.[31] In this way, Taíno genes have entered into the island's broad gene pool. Some researchers have claimed that present-day Puerto Ricans have inherited 61 per cent of their mitochondrial (female-transmitted) genes from the Taíno. This figure is highly debated, and other estimates suggest about 18 per cent for the "average" Puerto Rican. A recent study has shown links between ancient Taíno mitochondrial DNA, extracted from a female's tooth, and DNA of today's islanders.[32] Very little male Taíno DNA remains among Puerto Ricans. European and African contributions to the present-day gene pool coexist with Taíno. Of course, there is no "average" Puerto Rican, so these figures do not apply directly to individuals, and it is hard to link cultural practices to DNA composition. It is easy for anyone to claim Taíno ancestry and take pride in it, as do the proponents of Taíno "revivalism."[33]

Of greater interest for our purpose is the import of Taíno religious beliefs and practices to the religious history of Puerto Rico. Stevens Arroyo has argued that Taíno religion, because of its "predilection for the unconscious over the phenomenal world," "endowed the adherents with a marvellous capacity to merge their beliefs with those of other religions." The Taíno could incorporate Christian components into their religious practices and beliefs.[34] Some Taíno religious entities could correspond to the Christian Holy Trinity, the Virgin Mary, or the Devil. Catholic icons could be understood as having the same role and power as native cemís.[35] But the Spaniards repressed the Taíno *cohoba* ritual, which put its practitioners in a "trance" that enabled them to predict the future and thus make decisions for their community, because it was "the key institution of governance, of political and military decision making."[36] The encounter of Taíno and Catholic religious practices was the beginning of Puerto Rican religious syncretism, the unconscious or deliberate amalgamation of different religious traditions. Syncretism was not a one-way street: the popular veneration of Catholic religious images and the imploring of favours from the Virgin Mary and from the saints, such as the "Prayer to Win the Lottery,"[37] frowned on by Catholic theology, may be said to resemble the Taíno cult of the cemís. And, of course, the Taíno view of nature may be said to influence contemporary environmentalism. In Puerto Rican society today, Taíno religion and its successors had similar strategies for dealing with supernatural forces.

2

~

The Catholic Church in Spain,
16th–18th Centuries

As we have seen in the previous chapter, Taíno society had religious and political structures grounded in a worldview that united natural and supernatural. Religious and political structures were vested in the behique and the cacique, who exercised their power through ceremonies of consultation with the spirits, but with the implicit consent of their fellow Taíno. How different was sixteenth-century Spain? They look quite different, Spanish political and religious structures being much more rigid and compelling than their Taíno equivalent. Spanish forms of governance imposed in the New World would be incomprehensible to the native populations. Institutional forms of political and religious power – the state (monarchy) and the church, respectively, with their corporate rules and memory embedded in each bureaucracy – were alien to the oral social memory of the Taíno.

But perhaps sixteenth-century Spain appears as alien to our twenty-first-century perspective as to the Taíno. It is accepted in Canada and the United States that church and state should be separate, that belonging to a church is an individual choice, but following the rule of law imposed by the state is a citizen's basic obligation. In Spain, the rule of religion was as binding as the rule of the state. As with the caciques[1] in Taíno society, the political power of the Spanish monarchy claimed to derive from divine – supernatural – authority. Catholicism was the state religion, so the state controlled the Catholic hierarchy and enforced the practice of religion through various forms of coercion, up to and including torture and execution. However, the Catholic hierarchy held some moral sway over the monarchy, and the king's subjects sometimes had their own views on how to practise religion. The neat order of authority in Spanish society did not always apply without tensions or resistance; but such pushback did not have the same social legitimacy as objections to religious or political authority in Taíno society. Nevertheless, as the clergy's sway over the Spanish population varied from area to area, and as laymen had their own understanding of the power of God, Jesus, Mary, and the saints, popular religious beliefs and practices were often at odds with the church's. Local communities of the soul had their own dynamics and internal order.

A STATE RELIGION

Catholicism was the state religion of Spain, and after 1492 the only permitted religion. Spain itself was a creation of the fifteenth and sixteenth centuries, the result of the wedding in 1469 of Ferdinand II of Aragon and Isabel I of Castile and the annexation of Navarre in 1512. In the sixteenth century, Spain became a world power as its empire expanded from Europe to the Americas, Africa, Asia, and Oceania. It extended its language and its religion throughout its empire, including Puerto Rico.

The monarchs Ferdinand of Aragon and Isabel of Castile (and then the two jointly of Spain), and later Charles V and his son Philip II (reigned 1555–98), sought to enforce religious absolutism (*absolutismo confesional*), that every Spaniard should be a Roman Catholic.[2] This total religious uniformity (at least on paper) may be contrasted with the situation in France, where the Catholic–Protestant wars of religion were ended by the Edict of Nantes in 1598.

While Spain's Catholic hierarchy endeavoured to maintain its independence from Rome, the church had to support the crown financially and to bow to its power over the church's affairs.[3] In 1523, King Charles V obtained from Pope Adrian VI the right to appoint the bishops of his kingdom, but left the church to run its affairs, as he was mainly absent waging war against France and the Ottoman Empire.[4]

The Spanish Catholic church had considerable revenues. These came from tithe duties, rental of land, and mortgage interest. But seven-ninths of tithe revenue were turned over to the crown, which could also take money from bishoprics to pay pensions to "long-serving churchmen" and received income from other church activities; all of this represented a sizeable portion of the crown's annual revenue.[5] The financial ties between the church and the state meant that Catholicism was the state religion in practice as well as in theory.

Church and state sought to make Catholicism as prevalent as possible, both by expelling non-Catholics perceived as a threat to orthodoxy, and by attempting to convert those thought amenable.

Reconquest and Expulsions

In 1492, the joint monarchy of Aragon and Castile completed the Reconquista – the defeat of the Muslim Moors, who had ruled most of the Iberian peninsula for nearly eight hundred years, tolerating, even protecting Christians and Jews. It now ordered the Jews of the kingdom to convert to Christianity or be expelled. This completed a series of expulsions of Jews ordered by the Catholic Inquisition in Andalusia in 1483 and in Aragon three years later. Many Jews decided on outward conversion, and the exodus was much smaller than earlier studies have suggested. Discrimination, enforced segregation, confinement to ghettos, and heavy taxation had preceded these measures, all part of the monarchy's effort to enforce Catholic orthodoxy.

The imposition of religious uniformity continued ten years later when Queen Isabel ordered the expulsion of the Moors (Muslims) of Castile and León, "since there is much danger in the communication of the said Moors of our kingdom with the newly converted [who] may be drawn and induced to leave our faith and to return to their original errors ... as already by experience has been seen in some of this kingdom and outside of it," wrote the queen.[6] The remaining Moors, many of them highly skilled, provided a valuable workforce, but were considered a potential "fifth column" for an eventual Turkish attack on Spain.

The religious "homogenization" of Spain continued further a century later, in 1609, when Philip III ordered deportation of Muslims who refused to be baptized. The church justified the expulsion on religious grounds, because of "the dishonour suffered by true Christians through their forced coexistence with infidels and the need to placate God for having tolerated non-believers for so long."[7]

The Catholic hierarchy also sought to expose and expunge from its ranks any cleric suspected of holding Protestant leanings. Lutherans and Calvinists were hounded, even the learned Dominican Bartolomé Carranza, named archbishop of Toledo in 1658, whose trial for heresy lasted from 1561 to 1576. In some cases, exposed Protestants were burned at the stake, as happened in Valladolid and Seville in the late 1550s. There were just enough Protestants to inspire fear among Spaniards, and their presence had a paradoxical effect. "The Inquisition used the spectre of Lutheran heresy, rather than the real existence of it, to instil fear into the Spanish people and to reinforce its ideological control over them. The calculated campaign directed by the Holy Office in 1555–65, which reached its climax in the Valladolid and Seville *autos-da-fé* (burning people alive) of 1559–60, successfully prevented Protestantism from establishing a native root in Spain. As a result, it never posed a major threat to the religious stability of the Spanish kingdoms."[8]

CONVERTING THE INDIGENOUS PEOPLES

Expulsion was a simplistic solution to an old problem that the Catholic church in Spain had not effectively confronted: the evangelization of its non-Christian minorities. For centuries, Jews and Muslims had converted to Catholicism, but the authenticity of their conversion was often put in question. In fact, the Spanish Inquisition had been set up in 1480 to investigate Jewish *conversos*, or converts, suspected of reverting to the Jewish faith. In the sixteenth century, similar pressure was applied to the Muslims, who were numerous in the recently reconquered kingdom of Grenada, and who resisted, sometimes with violence, the pressure to convert. In all, nearly 300,000 *moriscos*, or Muslims supposedly converted to Christianity, were expelled between 1609 and 1611. "By forcing Jews and Moors to accept Christian baptism rather than integrating them via a full programme of instruction, the crown ensured that they would long remain reluctant converts."[9]

Given the Spanish crown's determination to turn Spain into a homogeneous Catholic kingdom, it is not surprising that the same determination would apply to the New World. Spain had begun its extraterritorial expansion in the Canary Islands, in the Atlantic off the coast of Africa, in 1341. "By 1492 Spain had spent more than a hundred years acquiring island possessions both in the Mediterranean (Balearic Islands) and the Atlantic (Canary Islands)," notes Stevens Arroyo. It had used settlement, military action, and the confinement of local populations into *repartimientos* – land and population granted as spoils of war – to extend its domination of the Canary Islands. The Spanish monarchy outlawed enslaving the Islands' natives and fostered their conversion, the justification used for its conquest of the islands. But conversion met resistance, as it would in the Caribbean, where Taíno society, ravaged by European diseases, would dissolve before conversion could take place.[10]

In 1508, the pope granted the Spanish crown complete control over the church in America, even over papal bulls and edicts. "In the Americas, it was the Spanish monarchy rather than the papacy that acted as the supreme head of the Catholic Church."[11] There was a sustained debate in Spain, within both church and state, about how to evangelize the "Indians" and the need to "civilize" them before they could be truly converted to Christianity. The use of force and the "reduction" of natives to communities under religious and military control often encountered criticism and resistance from the natives' defenders, since it benefited the Spanish landowning elite in the colonies.

On the Sunday before Christmas 1511, at the beginning of Spanish rule in the Caribbean, the Dominican friar Antonio de Montesinos, in a sermon in the church of Santo Domingo, the capital of Hispaniola, accused the parishioners of living in mortal sin because of the cruelty and tyranny they inflicted upon the native peoples. He repeated his accusations the following week, adding that such sinners would no longer be heard in confession or given communion. His parishioners complained all the way to the king, who ordered the governor to reason with Montesinos. A more direct reproach was sent by the Dominican superior in Spain to the Dominican provincial in Hispaniola, ordering the end of such "scandalous doctrine." The issue led to the "first comprehensive code of Indian legislation," the Laws of Burgos, drafted by a committee of theologians and ju-rists; it imposed Catholicism but set out regulations against ill treatment.[12]

The best known of the church's defenders of the American natives against exploitation, enslavement, and enforced conversion was Bartolomé de las Casas. One of the first Spanish colonizers of Hispaniola in 1502, Las Casas was a priest, a landowner, and a slave owner. He had heard Montesinos's sermon and had been unmoved by it. But in 1514 he was convinced by a reading of Ecclesiastes that enslaving the natives was illegal and a great sin.[13] He gave up his own slaves and began a life-long fight to convince the Span-ish monarchy of his views. He had some success, being named protector of the Indians, but was embroiled in an extended theological debate with other clerics, who argued that the natives were of inferior stock and had to be pacified and converted forcefully. This debate raised the issue of Spain's right to colonize America and the right to exploit native people and re-sources, so it was understandably heated and prolonged.[14]

Whether by slow, peaceful, individual conversion or by quick, mass bap-tisms, the Spanish missionaries in the New World attempted to inculcate Catholic religious practices among the natives. The church sent members of the regular clergy (members of a religious order), such as Franciscans, Dominicans, and Jesuits, to evangelize the natives in the Caribbean and on the American continent. The regular orders had the best-educated priests that could be deployed in the Spanish New World. But their views on the local population, and how to spread the Catholic faith, could differ sub-stantially. A Franciscan monk, Geronimo de Mendieta, and others in his order were ready to accept "the moderate use of coercion" in the pursuit of conversion, while Dominican theologians "usually minimized and often repudiated the principle of force." Mendieta considered the Spanish monar-chy mandated by God to "convert all of mankind on the eve of the Last Judgment." He and others recognized that "the Indians were defenseless in contact with the Spaniards."[15]

The missionaries attempted to replace the natives' rituals – for example, the veneration of ancestral idols – with Christian ones, such as devotions to saints.[16] In Puerto Rico these efforts had little success. The Taíno "abandoned Puerto Rico in large numbers rather than submit to Spanish subjugation." Those who remained had to accept the invaders' religion to

avoid forced labour. Taíno society disappeared after the smallpox epidemic
of 1518, even though some of its cultural traits persist in Puerto Rican society today.[17]

CATHOLIC CLERGY IN SPAIN

Catholicism in Puerto Rico arrived both with the regular clergy missionaries to the natives and the local Catholic hierarchy, and with the lay
Spaniards who settled on the island. Spanish migrants to Puerto Rico from
the sixteenth to the eighteenth centuries had learned Catholic doctrine and
practice from a Spanish clergy whose religious knowledge and behaviour
were patchy and sometimes tenuous. The church's institutional presence
on the island during the first centuries of colonization is the subject of the
next chapter. Here we explore the evolving situation of the Catholic clergy
in Spain, to reveal the religious environment in which Puerto Rico's lay
Spanish settlers had grown.

The clergy ran the church's business unevenly. Bishops, most of whom
had noble blood, sometimes put their lay duties, such as serving the
royal administration, ahead of their clerical ones. "The archbishopric
of Toledo – the highest ecclesiastical office in the Spanish Church – was almost exclusively held by an absentee servant of the crown in the early modern period." Bishops could be promoted to different sees over time, making
for relatively short periods of administration.[18] The size and distribution
of the fifty-five bishoprics and archbishoprics varied widely over the kingdom. They were "concentrated in northern Castile and Aragon, where the
roots of Christianity ran deepest, and were more thinly spread further
south, where Moorish civilisation had survived the longest. Toledo ... was
the largest archdiocese in Europe and the richest after Rome."[19] Differences
between north and south also applied to parishes. Three-quarters of the
twenty thousand parishes of late-sixteenth-century Spain were in northern
Castile – small, and thus poor, often with no resident priest. Conversely, in
the larger parishes of the south, there were so many souls to minister to
that "priests had little real contact with their parishioners."[20]

The church accordingly "exercised minimal influence" over the daily lives
of Spaniards, who managed their religious affairs as they saw fit. Religious

instruction was often lacking and left ample room for "superstition and ignorance," particularly in Galicia, the Basque country, and the remote Canary Islands.[21] To counter this ignorance, even among priests, for which the Council of Trent (1545–63) had mandated reform in clerical education, twenty seminaries were established in Spain in the second half of the sixteenth century, and a further eight in the seventeenth.

But this did not entirely solve the problem. "There remained profound regional variations in the standard of pastoral leadership to be found in post-Tridentine Spain. According to the findings of a recent study, reform never touched the clergy of Cantabria, the majority of whom regarded their office as a means of material gain. In 1580, half the clergy of Oviedo were still not versed in Latin or able to administer the sacraments ... Illiterate priests could still be found in rural Catalonia at the end of the seventeenth century. Friars were employed as preachers and confessors in certain areas to make up for the deficiencies of priests." Improvements in the training of priests spread unevenly. "Reform ... was essentially an urban phenomenon. At the local community level, ancient religious customs and traditions were not easily dislodged to make way for a centrally imposed and directed form of worship and belief. Huge areas of the peninsula remained beyond the disciplinary reach of reformers."[22]

The Spanish clergy was an influential and numerous "social class" with considerable influence over matters both religious and civil. At the beginning of Philip IV's reign in 1621, it was estimated that Spain had 70,000 regular priests and 30,000 seculars, numbers that doubled under his reign. Another estimate gives 200,000 priests at the beginning of the seventeenth century. In 1634, there were 9,088 monasteries for men, and the number increased considerably until the king's death in 1665. Madrid, in particular, was full of convents. There were too many priests for all of them to have the vocation of sacrifice or the elevated spirit required by their ministry. Their moral and intellectual levels were reputed lower than their predecessors' in the preceding century.[23]

Spanish clergy was often the source of complaints from bishops. For example, many priests were considered ignorant of Latin. Monasteries were a haven for lazy and ignorant men fleeing from work or military service. There were often conflicts between religious orders. The Dominicans were the enemies of the Franciscans and Augustinians. All had a low opinion of Jesuits. There were also conflicts about symbols of power between the clergy and representatives of civil authority, as illustrated by disputes over who would lead public processions.[24]

Neither was the clergy exempt from sins against its vows of chastity and poverty. Some members took mistresses, slept with married women, and perpetrated rape or pederasty. Some also accumulated material possessions, gambled, engaged in scams or theft, defied authority, and carried on thieving in gangs.[25]

Female members of religious orders were also the targets of complaints. Mundane and frivolous nuns outnumbered the virtuous. All kinds of social gatherings, including dances and comedy, could take place in the parlours of convents. But nuns were also victims of sexual exploitation by monks, such as a certain Capa, found guilty in Toledo of having had sex with 422 nuns.[26]

By the mid-eighteenth century, criticism against the ignorance and the weaknesses of the flesh exhibited by both regular and secular clerics continued, while popular religious practice remained ritualistic, marked by profane and "grotesque" public manifestations, the "excessive" adoration of statues and relics, and the "blind" belief in some miracles.[27] The Catholic hierarchy decried the nighttime parades and festivities that turned religious occasions into popular manifestations of what they considered debauchery. These went on anyway.[28]

RELIGION AMONG THE PEOPLE

The practice of popular religion included individual and collective beliefs and practices, some of which the Church approved and encouraged, as well as practices it condemned, such as superstitions and what it defined as sinful behaviour.

Beliefs and Rituals

Religious practices in Spain were not defined exclusively by the Catholic hierarchy. Local communities insisted on defining their own religious practices for local purposes – to avert disasters or to improve local conditions, for instance – or in memory of past local events. William A. Christian Jr, has drawn evidence for this from replies to a royal survey of 1575–80 of towns and villages of New Castile, which asked about "churches, benefices, relics, hermitages, miracles, feasts, monasteries, and hospitals." Christian insisted on the rootedness of collective religious practice in the local community, whether it be large or small, urban or rural.[29]

The answers to the survey questionnaire reveal religious beliefs often permeated with a "bargain with the gods" to obtain favours or to avoid disasters such as droughts or epidemics. This bargain was set out in vows made not only by individuals but by whole communities, which would then be bound by the vows. These collective vows could promise abstinence from meat-eating on the eve of a local holy day, or to hold a feast on the day itself, or both. They could seek protection from disease, from epidemics, or from natural disasters involving crops – infestations of grasshoppers, against which excommunication was practised – or of insects that attacked vines and forests, or drought.[30]

Many vows were for pilgrimages to shrines or chapels, or to construct and maintain a community's own shrine or chapel. The vows often "built and almost completely maintained most shrines and chapels, and still do" in modern-day Spain; they were, and are, "the quintessential institutions of local religion."[31] In sixteenth-century Spain, the best known of these were shrines to the Virgin of Guadalupe in Extremadura and to the Virgin of Montserrat in Catalonia. These two forms of Marian devotion became popular in the New World as well.

Processions were another form of communal "bargain with the gods." They could involve carrying saints' relics or images, or a walk from the community to the site of a shrine. They were held in the countryside and in large cities such as Barcelona and Seville to beg an end to droughts.[32]

Each community of course had its church's patron saint, and the celebration of the saint's feast day was a mandatory local holy day. But other saints could be "active" in the community, when, for instance, disasters such as pestilence struck. Communities "seem to have considered the saint on whose day a disaster occurred in some way the source of their misfortune; the saint was thought to be angry and to need placation, or else the saint was perceived as seeking devotion." Saints could be angry, but more often they were appealed to as intercessors. "Just as they paid their lawyers,

sometimes going into debt to do so, villages and towns entailed their resources in the form of future masses, penance, and work time to pay saints
to be their lawyers before God." But people's bad behaviour could also
provoke divine anger, and punishment would be meted out by God or his
angels.[33] Patron saints were the anchors of the parishes' communities of
the soul.

As saints could manifest their role, so too could holy images or statues.
Signs, whether from animals or strange lights, would indicate where to worship images or statues. Signals, such as the different rate of combustion of
candles, were used to select the saints a community should venerate on a
holy day.[34]

Veneration of saints declined after the sixteenth century, when they
mandated from thirty to forty holy days a year on top of the Sundays and
holy days decreed by dioceses; this amounted to about eighty-five days
a year when work was not allowed, except occasionally for bringing in
crops.[35] This was almost one day out of four and had an obvious impact
on productivity.

The increased popularity of Marian devotion in the sixteenth century
compensated for the decline in devotion to saints. Mary was believed to be
the most efficacious intercessor between a community and God. Devotion
to her was encouraged by the clergy, and "most Marian feast days were obligatory." Shrines to Mary, usually in the countryside, were said to be the site
of many miracles.[36]

The sixteenth century also witnessed the rise in veneration of Christ,
which would continue to grow till about 1800. This was particularly manifest in the creation of flagellant *cofradías* (brotherhoods), which became
very popular and would lead processions carrying crosses during Holy
Week.[37] Other types of brotherhoods proliferated, especially those devoted
to Mary – estimated to represent one-third of late-eighteenth-century
Spain's brotherhoods, which totalled over 25,000. These groups offered the
major channel of sociability in Spanish society, especially in rural areas.[38]

"Superstitions"

Communities' sharing of religious belief extended beyond the saints,
Mary, or Christ. According to a specialist on Spanish religious life, super-

stition in Spain in the seventeenth century became so prevalent that he dubbed it the major "health problem" of the period.[39] People believed in spells, amulets, apparitions, horoscopes, in the spiritual powers of the planets, or in ghosts that bothered the living in order to obtain favours of a religious nature.

Some material objects were believed to be endowed with specific magical powers. For example, the "miraculous" church bells of Velilla, in the province of Valladolid, would ring by themselves from time to time (twelve times in the seventeenth century) to foretell of extraordinary events, mostly unfortunate ones, such as defeat of the Spanish army.[40] Relics of the saints, which were objects of veneration by the church, were also used both by clergy and by laymen to "ward off storms, as well as to bring the rains and cure illnesses."[41] These beliefs and practices have obvious similarities to the Taíno's, suggesting they answered similar spiritual needs.

The devil was a source of popular superstition. He could cause violent storms and possess people. The clergy, too, believed in the devil, Satan, and in his acolytes, Lucifer and Beelzebub. Some possessions by the devil were deemed "fake" and the clergy had advice on how to distinguish between real and fake possessions. The devil could be countered by exorcism or by "white" magic, which one Jesuit publication considered superior to science.[42]

Belief in witchcraft, another form of the devil's work, took different forms and varied in intensity. During the reign of Philip III (1598–1621), witchcraft was particularly prevalent in the Basque region. Its practices were different in Castile and Andalucía from those in Navarre. Repression of it by the burning of witches also varied by region: the regional Inquisition tribunals in Toledo, which included Madrid, and in Córdoba condemned witches to physical punishment but did not burn any. Rioja and Navarre were less clement, and in Aragon and Cataluña, witches were put in prison, tortured, or put to death by hanging.[43] Witches, of course, were mainly women, many of whom were considered witches because they were *gitanas* (gypsies), but widows and prostitutes could also be accused of being witches.

The ancient belief in the "evil eye" was also common in Spain. The evil eye could cast spells; those who knew they had such an eye were to cover it with a patch to avoid inadvertently casting a spell. Some folks could remove spells with herbs, scents, and complicated ceremonies.

There were also rituals to avoid bad outcomes or to obtain good ones, such as getting rid of pain, winning at games of luck, or finding hidden treasures.[44] These practices, and their practitioners, recall the role and actions of the Taíno behique.

"Sinful" Behaviour

Before the Council of Trent (1545–63), the knowledge and practice of the basic tenets of Catholicism were very unevenly held among the Spanish population. Prayers, for instance, were taught by parish priests in Latin, which even some of the priests had trouble understanding. Sunday Mass, of course, was said in Latin, which precious few in attendance could follow. Its celebration was, for the community, a spectacle in which it took little part. Attending church on Sundays was more a social than a religious occasion, as the bishop of Mallorca ruefully noted in 1570: "His parishioners came to Mass halfway through and left before it was finished, talking and discussing their affairs throughout." He was not alone: in Oviedo, for instance, "Mass was often interrupted by violent disputes between members of the congregation," while in Burgos clergy could be insulted during Mass, especially by those whose behaviour the priest had denounced during his sermon.[45]

Local religious practice sometimes deviated from official Catholic theology. Sex among unmarried persons was not considered sinful, a belief for which the Inquisition would condemn large numbers of people in the last quarter of the sixteenth century. Peasants also resisted going to confession.[46]

After the Council of Trent, the knowledge and practice of Catholicism improved gradually, if unevenly. Learning the catechism from the parish priest on Sundays, being able to recite the Ten Commandments, attending Sunday Mass, and fulfilling the requirement of yearly confession became more widespread, but did not reach some of the more isolated or priest-deprived regions of Spain. As late as 1617, some parishes in the diocese of Avila had never received a visitation from the bishop, and confirmation was irregularly administered. The Inquisition made it its business to control more closely the behaviour of the Spanish population. "Popular ignorance and superstition now became criminal offences." Blasphemy and erroneous statements about the Catholic faith were subject to prosecution, fines, "lashes, or, in the more serious cases, public penance or imprisonment." This instilled a climate of fear and suspicion that would grow as the clergy extended its reach.[47]

The Spanish practice of Catholicism, at the time of the "discovery" of America and in the centuries that followed, was rudimentary and uneven. It was a state religion and became a heavier and heavier imposition on the Spanish population, but it remained largely what orthodox Catholicism would consider a shallow form of belief, marked by sparse knowledge of precepts and uneven adherence to the outward manifestations of the faith. The Spanish laity, however, took from Catholicism what it found appropriate, useful, or comforting, as it fashioned its own religious beliefs and practices. These were the practices that Spanish immigrants would bring to the New World.

3

~

The Catholic Church in Puerto Rico,
16th–18th Centuries

The Catholic religion arrived in Puerto Rico with the first Spanish ships. Columbus landed on the western coast of the island (there is a dispute as to where exactly, in Aguadilla or Aguada) in November 1493. It was on this trip to the Antilles that Columbus brought Brother Ramón Pané to Hispaniola. But Columbus did not undertake to settle Puerto Rico during this trip; he only stayed two days. The first Spanish settlements occurred in 1508 and in 1509, when Ponce de León brought about a hundred men to Caparra, in what is present-day Guaynabo, about 2.5 kilometres (1.5 miles) south of the bay of San Juan and close to the mountain streams that were believed to contain the alluvial gold the Spaniards sought to take back to Spain. Two years later, the first bishopric was created; it was the third bishopric in Spanish America, after the two in Hispaniola (Santo Domingo), where the Spanish first settled.

Alonso Manso, a priest at the Spanish court, was named bishop of San Juan. He arrived in 1513, the first Catholic bishop in America. He tried to build a small church in Caparra but lost all he had brought from Spain for the church when Taíno attacked the new settlement. He quarrelled with civil and military authorities and his flock and found he had few material resources to survive on (even with the 150 Taíno he was granted to work panning gold); he returned to Spain three years later, but returned in 1519, with the title of Inquisitor.[1] These beginnings foretold of recurrent themes in the church's history in Puerto Rico under Spanish rule. Clerical presence was scarce and intermittent; material resources to sustain the clergy were meagre; religious authority was contested both by civil powers and by the flock. These factors would account for much of the thinness of the links between the Catholic clergy and the island population outside the capital.

THE LATIN AMERICAN CONTEXT

The Puerto Rican church's structure of governance during Spanish rule depended on the arrangements the crown and the pope made between 1508 and 1512 to establish the church in Latin America. Broadly speaking, the pope granted the king the right to "recommend" the nomination of bishops, priests, and other religious dignitaries for approval by the pope. In practice, the papacy always accepted these recommendations. As well, the crown undertook the material support of the clergy: income provided by church tithes and other church revenues were to be collected under crown authority and shared between the government and the church. The crown would see to the creation of parishes and monasteries. These agreements bore the name of *Patronato Real* (royal patronage).[2] The Spanish crown would exercise even more power over the church in the colonies than in the metropolis. It was also entrusted with the conversion of natives to the Catholic faith.

The Patronato Real has its shortcomings, as the secretary of the Propaganda Fide, Cardinal Ingoli, noted more than a century later, in 1628. Clerics were ignorant of local idioms, dioceses and parishes were too large, and priests mingled in civil affairs, conducted businesses, and mistreated the natives. Ingoli recommended ordaining native clergymen. In 1644, he denounced the meddling of civil authorities in church affairs and the incompetence of colonial priests appointed by the monarchy.[3] His denunciations had little effect.

The devout King Fernando undertook the crown's religious duties, but they coexisted with his other responsibilities, including administering the colonies and fostering their economic development, which required local labour to exploit mines and for agriculture.

The easiest way to provide labour for the colonists was to enslave the native population. In Puerto Rico this was a short-lived option, as natives died from war or disease or fled to neighbouring islands or the mountains of the interior. Enslavement, of course, was a poor inducement to conversion into the Catholic faith. On the island of Santo Domingo, thousands of natives were said to have committed suicide by drinking the poisonous juice of the yuca plant, while native mothers aborted their fetuses or killed their children.[4] Nor did the bar to the ordination of natives as priests encourage participation in Catholic rituals.[5]

Importing slaves from Africa became the "solution" to the labour problem in the Caribbean and in Latin America. As slave ships arrived, Catholic priests tried to teach the rudiments of the Catholic faith to the slaves and to baptize them.[6] The obstacles to their conversion were similar to those affecting natives, but the latter died off while the African population eventually grew and resisted its white masters by keeping alive some of its own rituals of belief. At the end of the sixteenth century, Nicolas de Ramos, bishop of Puerto Rico, reported having discovered that Black men and women met every night to pray to the devil and renounce the Catholic God, the Virgin Mary, and the church's sacraments. Three Black women who refused to stop these practices were turned over to the civil authorities for punishment by *auto-da-fé* (burning alive) in front of the San Cristobal gate.[7] Similar incidents took place in the early seventeenth century. Clearly Afro-Caribbean religious practices were continuing,[8] although their collective manifestations remain undocumented.[9] In other cases, Africans assimilated Catholic veneration of saints to the veneration of their own deities and melded these rituals together, as some Taíno had done with their own and Catholic rituals.

LATIN AMERICAN POPULAR
RELIGIOUS PRACTICES

Spanish newcomers brought with them the popular religious practices of the home country, as Puerto Rican historian Salvador Brau noted long ago.[10] Whether or not the first catechisms printed in Latin America (in

Mexico, in 1546 and 1548)[11] reached Puerto Rico, for the illiterate population, religious instruction came mainly from oral sources such as priests – Franciscans and Dominicans, and later, Jesuits as well as secular clergymen – and nuns. The cult of the Virgin Mary was without doubt the most popular Catholic veneration in Latin America, particularly the Virgin of Guadalupe, who portrayed the "liberation" and "reconquest" of Spain from the Moors and made miraculous apparitions in Mexico.[12] Besides pilgrimages to Marian sanctuaries, Latin Americans also constituted cofradías (brotherhoods) for devotional, charitable, and social purposes,[13] like those so widespread in Spain.[14]

A LARGE AND THIN DIOCESE

A few years after the diocese of San Juan was created in 1511, its territory was extended to include the Windward Islands of the Lesser Antilles. This made the bishop's task even more arduous, and he seldom could visit all of his flock. There was also a lot of turnover: eight bishops between 1511 and 1599, fifteen in the seventeenth century, and fourteen in the eighteenth century.[15] Ten of the first fifteen incumbents were from a variety of religious orders.[16]

Given the scarce population of the island through that era, the creation of parishes was slow: in the sixteenth century, besides San Juan, only San Germán in the west (1512), Coamo in the south (1577, for about twenty Spaniards), and Aguada on the north-western coast (1692), and in the seventeenth, Arecibo on the north shore (1616), Hormigueros on the west coast (monastery created in 1646), and Ponce on the south shore (1680). Most of the other parishes today were eighteenth-century creations[17] (see figures 4.1 and 4.2).

The main primary sources for this period consist of official church documents, such as letters to the authorities in Spain, notes from pastoral visits, and the records of the synod of 1645, the period's only one. These sources offer little direct purchase on popular religious practice, but they do contain some useful indications.

SIZE AND QUALITY OF CLERGY

As the island's population grew, albeit slowly, so the clergy became more diverse. At the top of the hierarchy, the bishop and his assistants formed the *curia*, the administrative arm of the bishopric. In San Juan, the cathedral had a chapter of canons – priests who administered the cathedral and were also supposed to help the bishop in his ministry. This group was appointed by the Spanish crown, which provided for its material support. For instance, besides the Taíno whose labour he had been granted, the first bishop, Alonso Manso, was given fourteen African slaves in 1528.[18] He received the same emoluments as other Latin American bishops, or about 18,000 pesos per year. In comparison, the dean of the cathedral received five hundred pesos.[19] The bishop also received a quarter of the tithe collection, the cathedral chapter another quarter, and the rest was divided among parish priests, hospitals, churches, and their fabrics (the parishes' administrative entities), and the king of Spain.[20] Thus the church's material resources were concentrated in the capital city, leaving little material support for parishes and their curates. This situation did not make for a numerous clergy.

From the early days of the colony, regular orders opened convents in the colony. The Franciscans had a convent in Caparra by 1515. They arrived in San Juan in 1634 and obtained land for their convent on San Francisco Street in 1642.[21] The Dominicans had been the first regular order in San Juan, starting construction on their monastery in 1523.[22] They had a monastery and a church in San Juan (now known as the San José church, across from the Plaza del Quinto Centenario), and by 1582 about ten of them lived off alms and cattle ranching.[23] They were "preachers and confessors for the educated class"[24] but did not always see eye to eye with the local hierarchy. The second bishop of Puerto Rico, Rodrigo de Bastidas y Rodríguez de Romera, a secular priest, complained that the Dominicans were too prosperous, despite the order's vow of poverty.[25] The bishop fought over resources with them and lost, and left for Hispaniola.[26] In 1578 and 1579, Bishop Diego de Salamanca Polanco, an Augustinian, lamented that the Dominican priests were not well educated.[27]

Puerto Rican priests – the first ones were ordained in 1547 – made up most of the clergy in the sixteenth century, able to depend on their families, according to Stevens Arroyo,[28] while, as Bishop Salamanca noted in 1578, priests from the metropolis were unable to sustain themselves.[29] Later in the century, the bishops of San Juan considered the home-grown secular priests "extremely ignorant," showing, like most Spaniards, contempt for the *criollos*.[30] Bishops reiterated this complaint in the early seventeenth and early eighteenth centuries.[31]

The numbers of secular priests proved inadequate. The smallpox epidemic of 1689–90 killed twenty-five priests; in 1713, twenty-two parishes remained without priests. As late as 1760, Bishop Oneca counted only fourteen priests for a population of 37,923 souls, and only one candidate worthy of ordination.[32] Early in the colony's history, as we have seen, bishops recruited regular clergymen, to which a number of the bishops belonged. Dominicans and Franciscans preached around the island.[33] In the late eighteenth century, Bishop Jiménez Pérez acknowledged the positive effect of frequent missions by Franciscans and Dominicans, who sometimes served as parish priests for lack of secular clerics. Franciscans also taught Taíno and children of poor families in San Germán and in San Juan.[34] The clergy gave religious instruction to local Black slaves and to Blacks coming from Protestant colonies, the latter being granted their freedom if they joined the Catholic church. But some bishops refused to ordain Blacks as priests,[35] and at the end of Spanish rule this was still the practice, as Father Juan Perpiñá e Pibernat, ecclesiastical governor and capitular vicar of Puerto Rico, reported to US commissioner Henry K. Carroll in 1898: he argued that the "clerical constitution of Spain" forbade the practice. Carroll asked why, and Perpiñá's answer is revealing:

> Dr Carroll. What was the reason for the discrimination against coloured men in the priesthood?
>
> Father Perpiñá. I do not know the reason, but for myself I do not consider it desirable to see coloured men with priestly robes administering the sacraments, and if I were a bishop I would never ordain a coloured man.
>
> Dr Carroll. Is there a race prejudice that would prevent it?
>
> Father Perpiñá. There is none. There has always been, though, a breach between the coloured and the whites since the emancipation

of the slaves in the island. I think the coloured people have been conceded many more liberties than they should have received, and what
they have not been conceded they have taken.[36]

The role of priests, of course, was to dispense the sacraments and instruct
their flock in the faith. In 1760, Bishop Martínez de Oneda ordered parish
priests to teach catechism on Sunday afternoons for half an hour, under
threat of fines, as he had noticed many did not bother.[37]

This was not the clergy's only form of misbehaviour. In 1645, the new
bishop, Damián López de Haro, called a diocesan synod to "extirpate whatever abuses there are in our diocese."[38] The synod imposed many norms of
behaviour on priests, an admission of laxity. They were not to engage in
commerce, deal in land and crops, play dice, participate in "comedies,"
feasts, and dances, live with women, which might give rise to rumours, and
even work in the fields or in construction.[39] In 1706, Bishop Urtiaga noted
that the majority of his twenty-five priests did not meet minimal conditions
for their duties. In 1760, according to Bishop Martínez de Oneda, most of
the island's fourteen priests were too old or insufficiently trained.[40]

RELIGIOUS PRACTICES OF THE LAITY

Lay religious practice at times is autonomous from clerical authority, at
times amplifies accepted forms of worship, and at times is constrained by
physical distance from clerical personnel.

Most information on popular religious practice comes from church documents, and we may assume that the hierarchy would stress the laity's fail-
ings in order to obtain more resources for their pastoral duties. But its
observations are remarkably similar across the period, and accounts by visitors to the island often support them. Ángel López Cantos examined 2,647
civil and criminal cases during the eighteenth century, and his findings cor-
roborate those from church documents on religious practices.[41]

For many Puerto Ricans in rural areas, or even in smaller towns, attending Sunday Mass or even going to Mass at Easter was not easy: they needed
to work, and there were few priests or roads, so that from 1645 on rural folks
needn't attend Sunday Mass if they resided six leagues (a six-hour walk) or
more from a church, but had to attend Mass four times a year, at least at
Christmas and at Easter.[42]

There were many occasions to attend church. Besides Sundays, the feast days of the saints – all the feasts of the Virgin Mary, the apostles, and the "great saints" – totalled more than forty. But sugar-cane producers needed workers during the Christmas holidays, and absenteeism lessened attendance at religious holidays.[43]

Extreme poverty also prevented church attendance. Some parishioners went about half-naked,[44] as Bishop López de Haro noted at his arrival in 1644: "Many persons miss Mass on feast days because of lack of clothes to go to Church in, and in the fields they go about naked and barefoot; this is the case not only for Negroes and Mulattos, even in the city, but also for many white women who don't cover their flesh with anything."[45] His successor, Francisco de Padilla, noted the same thing in 1688, asking the king for money to supply poor women with clothing so they could go to church.[46]

The same factors kept many people from the sacraments that mark a person's stages in life. The lack of priests led midwives to baptize the newborn.[47] Bishops would confirm many parishioners during pastoral visits[48] and hear confessions, normally the task of a parish priest: the synod of 1645 required parishioners to demonstrate their knowledge of Christian doctrine and to go to confession in their own parishes. Apparently, some of the faithful were "shopping" for more amenable clerics than their parish priest. The synod also reserved the absolution of some sins to the bishop: theft, superstition, blasphemy, homicide, abortion, incest, sodomy, bestiality, perjury, but also failure to pay tithe or assault on a member of the clergy.[49]

Marriage was a sacrament often honoured in the breach. Fees, dispensation re consanguinity, and prior confession and communion all posed obstacles, leading to frequent common-law arrangements.[50] This became part of the *jíbaro* (rural folk) culture. Unlike the sacraments of baptism and burial, which formally made one a child of God here and hereafter, and were thus essential to salvation, common-law marriage, or *amancebamiento*, appears to have been perceived as a minor offence. There could always be time for a religious wedding or, if not, for confessing the sin.

There were other ways to violate the sacrament of marriage. In 1798, the bishop asked for married Spaniards and foreigners who took up concubines to be deported. The civil authorities refused to act.[51]

Funeral services and interment in consecrated ground were the symbolic end to one's life on earth and the recognition of one's entrance into Heaven, with or without some time in Purgatory to atone for any remaining sins. At the 1645 synod, when there were few parishes on the island, fees were set for different levels of funeral services and burial ceremonies. The fees pertained to burials in the San Juan cathedral. Cemeteries were divided into three sections, by socio-economic class. Likewise, fees varied per type of funeral service and burial to be provided. A solemn ceremony, with Mass and a sung vigil, cost fifty-eight silver *reales*; a complete ceremony cost eighteen reales; burial of a child of less than eight years cost thirteen reales. On top of this, the parish fabric was to receive twelve reales, eight for the burial and the rest for the mourners, and each priest three reales. Some people avoided paying burial fees by burying their dead, particularly slaves, in the desert. Others apparently "shopped around" for burial in a parish, as the synod required burying the dead in their parish or, if not, paying the fees to their parish anyway.[52] Still others solemnly declared themselves poor, and thus avoided funeral services and burial fees.[53]

So, for various reasons, parishioners did not always follow the church's precepts concerning the sacraments. But they manifested their beliefs in the power of the supernatural by their devotion to the Virgin Mary and to the saints by popular practices in their parish church, in the public space, or at home in private. Praying to the Virgin Mary for favours or to intercede on one's behalf was probably the most popular of devotions and certainly one of the earliest. The Virgin of Montserrat, patron saint of Catalonia, was said to have kept alive an eight-year-old girl in the late sixteenth century who had been lost for two weeks in the woods around Hormigueros. The girl was the daughter of Gerardo González, a Hormigueros landowner of Catalan origin who, in thanks for his daughter's safe return, built a sanctuary in honour of the Virgin of Montserrat, to whom he was used to praying. After his wife's death, González became a priest and maintained the sanctuary. That the synod of 1645 saw González as chaplain of that very chapel suggests a later date for his story.[54] González became an ardent publicist for the Marian cult.[55] The Hormigueros shrine eventually became a church, and in 1998 the pope designated it a minor basilica.[56] Other Marian shrines were erected, for example in Coamo in 1685, as thanks for ending a cholera outbreak two years earlier.[57]

The shrines were but the most spectacular aspects of Marian devotion. Beginning in 1512, Saturday Mass was dedicated to the "honour and glory" of the Virgin Mary, a practice formalized by the 1645 synod.[58] But outside the church, public space was also a locus of Marian devotion. In the late eighteenth century, a visitor to the island noted bi-weekly public evening processions of the rosary, led by brothers who sang litanies and played the guitar.[59] Another observed that Puerto Ricans wore rosaries around their neck and recited the rosary at least twice a day.[60]

Prayers to the Virgin Mary were also held in private homes. In 1774, after a pastoral visit of his diocese, Bishop Manuel Jiménez Pérez forbade, under pains of a fine, home meetings of the faithful – men and women together – to recite or sing the rosary as a promise made in exchange for a favour from the Virgin. Some of these priest-less gatherings turned into large, all-night parties, where people gambled, danced, and drank. If these events took place on the eve of a feast day, many participants missed Mass the following day. This communal appropriation of religious rites for various purposes stoked the clergy's fear of losing control over manifestations of piety.[61]

From its earliest days, the Puerto Rican church encouraged devotion to specific saints. John the Baptist was the patron saint of the island, which was originally named San Juan de Puerto Rico. St Germain, selected in honour of Germaine de Foix, Ferdinand II's French-born second wife became the patron saint of the island's second parish, which comprised its western half. The third saint was Patrick. An infestation of insects had ruined the manioc crop during Manso's tenure as bishop, and the locals, following a Spanish custom, put all the saints' names in a bag and drew one – Patrick's. Not being familiar with him, they tried again, and twice his name came up. Taking this as a sign, the bishop ordered a yearly celebration of St Patrick, with Mass, sermon, and procession. A second infestation of the crop in 1641 was ended after a series of celebrations in honour of St Patrick.[62]

Of course, new parishes chose a patron saint, whom they honoured each year, a tradition that continues today. But there were also "specialist" saints for various problems or situations. Difficult or desperate cases were submitted to St Rita; the blind invoked St Lucy, those giving birth St Raymond Nonnatus (who was born by caesarean section), travellers St Christopher, builders St Vincent Ferrer, while St Martha protected homes and St Augustine consoled grief-stricken mothers.[63]

The lay faithful also joined cofradías set up for collective prayer and self-help. One dedicated to Marian devotion was set up in San Germán in 1582.

Similar groups had appeared in San Juan by the mid-seventeenth century. A cofradía of the Souls, which prayed for the souls in purgatory, had twenty-four members. It had a special Mass, with procession and sermon.[64] By 1645, the brotherhoods had become so numerous that the synod feared they would confuse the faithful, so it required the bishop's approval to set them up.[65] Some, such as the Brotherhood of the Conception, in Coamo in 1661, or that of the Souls, in Arecibo in 1720, were the bishop's creation on his pastoral visit.[66] For the eighteenth century, López Cantos found in practically every parish brotherhoods venerating the Holy Sacrament.[67] In 1798, the bishop's pastoral visit revealed ninety-seven cofradías, honouring the sacraments, the Virgin, the souls of the blessed, and specific saints.[68] They provided social interaction as well as devotion.[69]

Like recitations of the rosary in private homes, the activities of the cofradías could turn to the profane: a pastoral letter of 1712 condemned those content only to pay a Mass for their saint, while spending the rest of the funds they collected on dances, comedies, banquets, races, and sinful activities.[70] The faithful, once again, mixed devotion and amusement, or used devotion as a pretext for entertainment, depending on the depth of their religious beliefs. Communities of the soul were also communities of the flesh.

"SINFUL" BEHAVIOUR

Puerto Rico's Catholic hierarchy was aware of its flock's incomplete adherence to the church's precepts. The synod of 1645 addressed the two main "vices" of the faithful: failure to marry before the church and absence from Sunday Mass.[71] More than a hundred years later, in 1760, Bishop Martínez de Oneca attributed the prevalence of rape, adultery, common-law living, delinquency, and lack of a work ethic to the dispersion of the population and to the difficulties of travel.[72] Bishops used pastoral visits to inquire about parishioners' habits and to condemn and repress heretics or the immoral. As in Spain, sins were civil offences and sinners criminals.

But civil repression of "sinful" behaviour had its limits, particularly when both civil and religious authorities engaged in the same behaviour. An example would be prostitution. The civil authorities considered whorehouses an instrument for maintaining public order, but the church severely condemned pimps. Ideally, prostitutes were to ply their trade without them. In 1526, the Spanish crown authorized the opening of a whorehouse in San Juan. Prostitution was tolerated from the sixteenth to the eighteenth century.[73] Sins of the flesh were deemed to be a common occurrence.[74]

The first two centuries of Catholicism in Puerto Rico established a religious culture that, as elsewhere in Latin America, reproduced many elements of its Spanish template. The scant population and its poverty made it difficult for the church to extend its influence over the whole island. A certain social distance developed between the clergy and the faithful from the physical distance that separated them. Popular practices and beliefs evolved out of this distance and set the stage for a more turbulent nineteenth century.

4

Religious Counter-Revolution in Puerto Rico, 19th Century

THE SPANISH CHURCH CONTEXT

Like most other European countries, Spain in the nineteenth century experienced the struggle of liberalism against the old political and religious order, which began with occupation by Napoleon's armies 1808–14 and produced civil war, swings between liberal and reactionary government, and eventually parliamentary supremacy. Turmoil at home reverberated overseas, and by the mid-1820s Spain lost its vast American empire, except for Cuba and Puerto Rico. The church was caught in this turmoil: its struggles with the state and with anti-clerical liberals and other free thinkers diminished its material resources and enfeebled its clergy. These events, of course, affected Puerto Rico.

As Napoleon's armies entered Spain in late 1807 on their way to Portugal, the Spanish monarchy was threatened and had to abandon the throne to Napoleon's brother Joseph. Thus began was has been called the war of Spanish independence, which was in large part a guerrilla resistance to the French invaders. In the south of Spain, local authorities banded into juntas, taking over political and military authority, and in 1810 they gathered at Cádiz into a Regency Council in the forced absence of the king. This council in 1812 drafted a constitution that recognized the sovereignty of the nation (rather than of the king), constitutional monarchy, abolition of seigneurial tenure, universal male suffrage, freedom of the press, and the right to property; it also ended the Inquisition. Although the constitution confirmed Catholicism as the state religion, it contained the germs of liberalism that would challenge absolutist rule during the rest of the century.[1] In September 1813, the Cortes nationalized the properties of the Jesuit order and those of vacant convents and monasteries.[2] In 1814, Napoleon put back on the throne Ferdinand VII, who declared the Cádiz regency illegal and repealed the 1812 constitution. A specialist on the Spanish church of the period sets the metropolitan stage:

> The end of the liberal experiment in 1814 did not resolve the fundamental constitutional and ecclesiastical questions posed for the first time at the Cortes of Cádiz. The struggle between liberalism, determined to mold the Church to fit the demands of a new secular outlook within the framework of a parliamentary system, and ecclesiastical interests, as firmly committed to recover every particle of clerical authority and privilege, continued with even more intensity. The balance shifted first to the Church, during the initial period of Ferdinand VII's absolute rule from 1814 to 1820, and then against it during the second liberal revolution from 1820 to 1823. Although the Church recovered its position following the second restoration of Ferdinand, political and dynastic circumstances between 1823 and the king's death in 1833 finally ended ecclesiastical hopes for the reestablishment of the Old Regime Church in all its splendour. The clergy, at least the vast majority, struggled to recreate the past with the same fierce energy it had directed against the French and the constitutionalists of Cádiz. But the consensus that had sustained the eighteenth-century monarchy and the Church itself could not be resurrected. The Church threw its resources into a losing contest for which it would pay a heavy price.[3]

In the short term, the king helped the church to get rid of liberal-leaning clerics by banning them from benefices or even by arresting and imprisoning them, as in the case of the canon Joaquín Lorenzo Villanueva, a proponent of a vernacular Bible and prominent member of the Junta Central of Cádiz. But the church's problems ran deep. It had fewer resources for charitable work, it had lost regular priests during the war and was unable to replenish those ranks, and the secular clergy was often of questionable quality, as two bishops remarked in 1816: some priests lived with their female housekeepers or servants, others were drunks, others still said Mass "without devotion or any awareness of what they were doing." A "distinctly popular urban anticlericalism" emerged in the early 1820s and led the church to focus more on the countryside.[4]

The fight for political control resumed with violence after the king's death in 1833. The absolutists, headed by his brother Carlos, sought to overthrow the government of his widow, María Cristina, who became regent (their daughter, Isabel, was only three), supported by liberal reformers. Under María Cristina, liberals managed to hold on to power and instituted political and economic reforms, eliminating male religious orders, ending restrictions on female ones, and seizing the disbanded orders' properties. In 1837 the state abolished the tithe, which supported the secular clergy, and replaced it with a meagre salary. It also deadlocked with the papacy about naming bishops, so that by 1840 only eleven of the sixty dioceses had bishops, and none in the major cities. In 1841, the Cortes ordered the sale of the secular clergy's holdings to service the national debt. This was continued in 1855 and extended to the church's educational and charitable institutions.[5]

With monasteries gone, state and papacy agreed, in an 1851 concordat, on state-supported seminaries to train priests. This ended the "centuries-old tradition of theological education in the universities" and introduced "an abbreviated course of study designed to produce as many priests as possible within a short time," providing little pastoral training. But the regular orders – Augustinians, Dominicans, Franciscans, and Jesuits – obtained permission to train clergy for service in Cuba, Puerto Rico, and the Philippines.[6]

Religious practice in Spain was framed in two unequal ways. First, the rites practised by the clergy were often rote-based, and some priests celebrated "hasty Masses lacking in devotion," while others did not bother with Communion or sermons. Still, failure to receive Communion at Easter was rare, estimated at between 1 and 6 per cent of the population for 1828–43, for instance. Second, the church was less prone than in the preceding century to condemn lay forms of devotion; it accepted "miraculous" happenings reported by lay people and encouraged popular devotion to the Sacred Heart, to the Eucharist, and to the Virgin. "The folkloric customs of 'popular' religion – placatory in nature and connected to the fears and preoccupations of an uneducated peasantry – continued in the forms of local shrines, pilgrimages, and rites designed to evoke intercession to remedy specific ills ... To the peasantry, for whom religion warded off disaster and secured good fortune, the intercessionary aspects of devotion complemented rituals of traditional 'popular' religion, which often had little to do with formal belief."[7]

In the 1840s, Rome encouraged missions to the Spanish countryside, to give instruction in the catechism using new versions that made doctrine easier to comprehend. Devotional literature emphasizing individual salvation became popular. In late 1868, right-wing Catholics formed the Association of Catholics "to propagate and defend the doctrines, institutions, and social influence of the Church, particularly its liberty and the Catholic unity of Spain ... through peaceful means and under the protection of the law."[8]

The first two-thirds of the nineteenth century saw challenges to the moral authority of the Spanish church. During the war of independence, and again in the early 1820s, Freemason societies of French or British inspiration were founded in Spanish cities, their members numbering in the thousands by 1823.[9] In the 1830s, English Bible societies began disseminating Protestantism in Spain. During the turbulent early 1840s, various incidents of disrespect for Catholic ceremonies forced local authorities to intervene. To combat the substantial liberal press, the Catholic hierarchy launched new press organs that gave its clergy "a sense of unity and purpose."[10]

EXPANSION OF PARISHES AND BISHOPRICS

Even as Spain's South American colonies freed themselves in the 1820s and 1830s, Puerto Rico remained a strategic holding in the New World. Spain opened commerce in Cuba and Puerto Rico to traders from outside the Spanish empire and allowed European Catholic immigrants to settle on the islands. Sugar plantations developed, and African slaves were imported to work them. As the economy grew, so did the population, and the number of parishes[11] (see figures 4.1 and 4.2).

In 1800, the population was assessed at 155,000 in thirty localities (*partidos*).[12] By 1846, it had risen to 443,000, and by 1877 to 731,000.[13] By 1900, the number of localities had more than doubled.

Thirty-three churches were built all over the island between 1800 and 1850, sixteen of them dedicated to the Virgin Mary, suggesting the mass devotion to her. Five took the name Nuestra Señora del Carmen, four that of Inmaculada Concepción, two Nuestra Señora de la Monserrate, and one Nuestra Señora de la Guadalupe, these last two names recalling popular shrines in Spain and Mexico.

Until about 1850, communications across the island were difficult, relying mainly on coastal navigation. A structured postal service began in 1866, and island-wide telegraph service in 1874.[14] Difficult travel impeded monitoring of parish priests and their flocks. Thus confirmation, a bishop's prerogative, occurred only during infrequent pastoral visits: Utuado, for instance, had no such occasions between 1832 and 1852, when the bishop confirmed 5,876 people.[15]

San Juan lacked a bishop from 1833 to 1846. A seminary established there in 1832 produced only four priests out of the forty-five who entered between 1832 and 1847. The seminary closed in 1852, and the island recruited Spanish priests; between 1878 and 1883, the reopened seminary produced about two dozen ordinations. In the 1840s, the acting bishop of San Juan, Dionisio González de Mendoza, noted that very few island parishes were looking for priests, so a sustainable living was open to very few curates. A lucrative and prestigious clerical appointment to the cathedral chapter was largely closed to natives of the island.[16] Government seizure of the monasteries for revenue in 1837–38 reduced clerical resources.[17] The fact that priests had to be white males born in church-sanctioned wedlock further restricted recruitment.[18]

As in Spain, priests in Puerto Rico were paid by the state under the provisions of the Patronato Real. In 1815, however, the governor transferred the task to parishioners. The salaries were set at three hundred pesos per year;[19] by 1900, this figure had more than doubled.[20] The last Spanish budget for

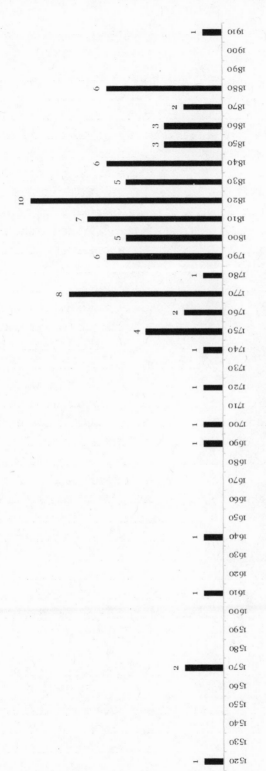

Figure 4.1 Parish churches started by decade, Puerto Rico, 1520–1910.

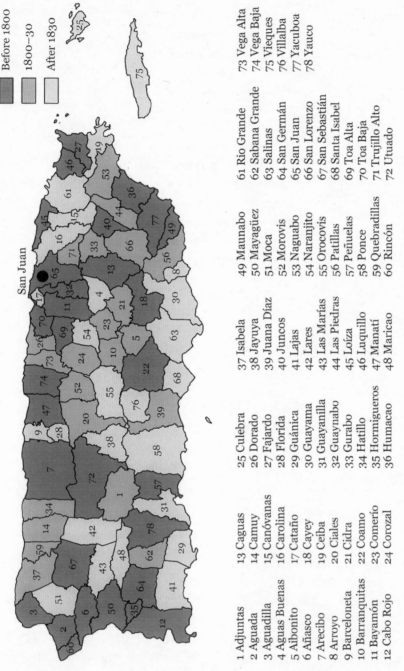

Figure 4.2 Periods of parish church construction, Puerto Rico, 1520–1910.

Before 1800
1800–30
After 1830

San Juan

1 Adjuntas	13 Caguas	25 Culebra
2 Aguada	14 Camuy	26 Dorado
3 Aguadilla	15 Canóvanas	27 Fajardo
4 Aguas Buenas	16 Carolina	28 Florida
5 Aibonito	17 Cataño	29 Guánica
6 Añasco	18 Cayey	30 Guayama
7 Arecibo	19 Ceiba	31 Guayanilla
8 Arroyo	20 Ciales	32 Guaynabo
9 Barceloneta	21 Cidra	33 Gurabo
10 Barranquitas	22 Coamo	34 Hatillo
11 Bayamón	23 Comerío	35 Hormigueros
12 Cabo Rojo	24 Corozal	36 Humacao

37 Isabela	49 Maunabo	61 Río Grande
38 Jayuya	50 Mayagüez	62 Sabana Grande
39 Juana Díaz	51 Moca	63 Salinas
40 Juncos	52 Morovis	64 San Germán
41 Lajas	53 Naguabo	65 San Juan
42 Lares	54 Naranjito	66 San Lorenzo
43 Las Marías	55 Orocovis	67 San Sebastián
44 Las Piedras	56 Patillas	68 Santa Isabel
45 Loíza	57 Peñuelas	69 Toa Alta
46 Luquillo	58 Ponce	70 Toa Baja
47 Manatí	59 Quebradillas	71 Trujillo Alto
48 Maricao	60 Rincón	72 Utuado

73 Vega Alta	
74 Vega Baja	
75 Vieques	
76 Villalba	
77 Yacuboa	
78 Yauco	

its Puerto Rican colony, in 1897–98, allowed $124,940 for the island's 158 priests, for an average of $970 each. However, thirty-four parishes did not have a resident priest at that date.[21] Municipal or state subsidies helped fund construction of some of the parish churches, so after the American conquest, some municipalities claimed that the buildings belonged to them and not to the church, as in Aibonito, Arroyo, Caguas, Cayey, Coamo, Guayama, Humacao, Ponce, and Yacuboa.[22]

By the end of Spanish rule, the population stood at 890,820,[23] and there were 137 parish priests (only thirty-four of them island-born)[24] – on average one priest for every 5,602 parishioners. By comparison, Catholics in the province of Quebec, in Canada, had a priest for every 680 parishioners.[25]

LOCAL CLERGY UNDER SUSPICION

The scarcity of island-born priests reflected not only lack of training facilities and poor pay, but distrust by imperial authorities and the church in Spain of native-born Latin American priests in general as the independence movements swept the region. The island's first native-born bishop (and the only one during Spanish rule), Juan Alejo de Arizmendi de La Torre, ordained six seminary students from Caracas after Venezuela declared independence in 1810.[26] This provoked suspicion in Spain, since he had, the previous year, publicly endorsed Puerto Rico's election of Ramón Power y Giralt, a liberal and nationalist navy officer, to the Cortes of Cádiz, even entrusting him with his episcopal ring.[27] One of Arizmendi's successors, Pedro Gutiérrez De Cos, a monarchist who had fled Peru after independence and became bishop in 1826, was mandated to reconcile his new flock to the Spanish metropolis.[28] In the 1840s, governors carried out a "clear political offensive" against *criollo* priests and their role in municipal elections, where, they argued, these priests supported independence.[29]

In 1870, a vicar of San Germán, José A. Pierretti, lost his posting because of his connection to the independence advocate Ramón Emeterio Betances, who had organized the 1868 popular uprising in Lares, in the west of the island.[30] The same year, a judge proposed that *peninsulares* (persons of Spanish birth) direct religious and civil education, to avoid contamination of youth by subversive ideas.[31]

As metropolitans were wont to do, the ecclesiastical hierarchy held a low opinion of criollo clergymen. It considered Puerto Rican priests ignorant, promiscuous, and leaning towards political independence, noted a canon.[32] They sometimes failed to administer the sacraments; some, like the curate of Isabela, Andrés Avelino Román, openly cohabited with their mistresses.[33]

THE "INVASION" OF PENINSULAR PRIESTS

To forestall any clergy-led independence movement, the Spanish crown named Spanish-born candidates as parish priests. These nominees fought anti-imperial sentiment, sometimes calling it anti-Christian.[34] With this attitude, its economic exploitation of the local people, and its defence of slavery – some owned slaves[35] – the Spanish-born clergy distanced itself from its flocks.[36] Also exploiting locals was the first long-term curate of Utuado, Don Calixto Vélez Borrero, born in Isabela, on the north-west corner of the island, the most prominent landholder in the parish and a slave owner; he seldom gave sermons or taught catechism.[37]

Priests in Puerto Rico came from various classes – indeed, from several countries – unlike the case in some other nineteenth-century Catholic societies. In Quebec, for instance, most clerics were locals, more than a third of them from farm backgrounds and a quarter from the artisan class, much as in France.[38] In Ireland, most domestic recruits hailed from farming families.[39] Agricultural upbringings and similar social provenance related priests in Quebec and Ireland to their flocks much more than was the case in Puerto Rico.

POPULAR RELIGIOUS PRACTICES

As we saw above, physical and social gaps between clergy and laity hampered religious instruction and administration of sacraments. Bishops' rare pastoral visits, noted Fernando Picó, provided sacraments such as confirmation.[40] Similarly, the scarcity of priests impeded interaction with parishioners except in the larger towns; in 1848, for example, the governor authorized in San Juan the celebration of Sunday retreats, reserving two hundred seats in the city's *plaza mayor* (main square) for use by the public.[41]

As in earlier centuries, many ordinary people's avoidance of church marriage upset the upper clergy, as well as civil authorities. People found the priest's fees onerous; Father Picó called marriage the "most expensive and most traumatic" of the sacraments – costing perhaps a day labourer's monthly income.[42] Also, episcopal dispensations for marriage by cousins in the second or third degree, not uncommon in rural areas, were expensive. Gil Estéve y Tomás, the island's bishop 1849–53, ordered marriages free of charge for *pobres de solemnidad* (persons officially recognized as poor) and personally performed "thousands" during his pastoral visits.[43] This was after the authorities advocated treating common-law spouses as vagrants, subject to regulations that, among other things, restricted freedom of movement.[44] This official crackdown was repeated in the 1850s and 1860s,[45] but did little to change popular behaviour.

One result was the high number of "illegitimate" (common-law) children. Father Picó noted that in 1868, 41 per cent of children baptized in Humacao, on the eastern shore, were born out of wedlock. The rate was 40 per cent in the capital, where the visible presence of the Catholic hierarchy did little to spur formal marriages.[46] This could have serious consequences, as "illegitimate" men could not become priests or government officials.

Among the laity in the early nineteenth century, as before, devotion to the Virgin Mary was omnipresent. In 1798, Bishop Juan Batista de Zengotita, a member of the Order of the Blessed Virgin Mary of Mercy, enjoined the curate of Porta Coeli, the church of the San Germán Dominican monastery, to recite the rosary daily to "excite the fervour, affection, and devotion of the faithful towards that Mother of Mercy" after the British attack on the colony the previous year.[47] The Virgin Mary was seen, in much of Latin America and the Caribbean, as a mediator between human beings and God.[48] The price of obtaining her favours was often a sung rosary, perhaps accompanied by guitars, maracas, or other instruments, which bishops had difficulty condoning.[49] In 1861, the chapter of the San Juan cathedral decreed 8 December the feast of the Immaculate Conception – "the object of great veneration, as patron saint of the Spanish monarchy."[50]

From earlier periods also persisted forms of popular practice relating to nature, à la the "bargains with the gods" common in Spain as well. A prominent doctor and liberal intellectual, Francisco del Valle Atiles, noted in his

1887 description of Puerto Rican peasants that prayers and religious medals were used as amulets against disease or the evil eye, which he considered "absurd forms of devotion" due to ignorance.[51] But in fact, remarked Fernando Picó, the church showed some opening to popular religious practices, allowing for domestic altars to the saints, wakes for the Three Kings (6 January), rosaries to the Holy Cross with singing and music,[52] vows for favours and religious dress as thanks for favours obtained, or traditional celebrations of the Christmas season, Holy Week, or the feast of a patron saint. It also arranged public processions and inserted dramatic touches in church ritual,[53] following metropolitan Spain.[54]

The history of the Catholic Church as an institution in nineteenth-century Puerto Rico was one of paradox. As it established close to fifty parish churches, and thus its physical proximity to the faithful, it became more jsuspicious of criollos as potential supporters of autonomy, even independence, and some exploited parishioners financially as moneylenders, slave owners, or landholders. It was also suspicious of popular religious practices, even while it tolerated their manifestations and engaged in more theatrical public demonstrations of devotion.

The formal creation of parishes and their attendant liturgical and devotional activities provided a forum for parishioners' sense of religious community, as attested to by brotherhoods and public recitations of the rosary, and this sense of religious community intermingled with awareness of social community.

By the 1870s and 1880s, the church was facing a growing number of heterodoxies, forced to share the public ideological space with them.

5

~

Challenges to Orthodoxy, 1870–1900

The last third of the nineteenth century saw the Catholic church's ideological supremacy in Puerto Rico begin to erode. As population increased from 731,648 in the 1877 census to 894,302 twenty years later,[1] it also became more closely interwoven, with a postal service starting in 1866 and telegraphic lines in the 1870s linking people across the island and with Europe and the Americas.[2] The population diversified: alongside migrants from various regions of Spain, French and Italian immigrants, nominally Catholic, brought different ways of thinking and living. The French seemed indifferent to religion, even critical of the clergy, dogmas, and church rites. Young Puerto Ricans returning from studies abroad brought with them books and newspapers that could spread notions of liberalism questioning religious beliefs.[3] Commerce brought not only foreign goods, but also new ideas in Spanish- and English-language publications.[4] Freemasonry and Protestantism also challenged the church's intellectual domination.

Nationalists included the liberal claim for freedom of religion in their political demands. In November 1867, Ramón Emeterio Betances, who was to lead the Grito de Lares insurrection the following year, defined the "Ten Commandments of Free Men" in a proclamation enumerating the conditions Spain needed to meet to keep the loyalty of Puerto Ricans: "*libertad de cultos*" (freedom of religion) came third, after abolition of slavery and the right to vote all taxes.[5] In 1869, under the new Spanish constitution, they would get their wishes, if only for a few years.

These challenges provoked reactions from both church and state. In 1875, the governor, General José Laureano Sanz y Posse, forbade "any attack on morals and religion, or on the sacred persons of authority in the Church," aiming specifically at the press. Eight years later, a tribunal in Ponce condemned the author of an article considered offensive to the church to a six-month jail term.[6]

THE SPANISH REPUBLIC AND RELIGIOUS LIBERALIZATION

The 1869 Spanish constitution, the product of the "Glorious" revolution of September 1868, brought constitutional monarchy to Spain. It guaranteed freedom of religion "without any limits but the universal rules of morals and law." This was restricted in 1875 after the return of the monarchy the previous year: freedom was replaced by "tolerance."[7] Even under the Spanish constitutional reform of 1897, Catholicism remained the state religion, and article 11, while it protected the free expression of religious opinion and the practice of faiths other than Catholicism, also required respect for Christian morality.[8]

The Spanish government under the constitution of 1869 made changes to the Real Cédula of 1858 and made municipal governments paymasters for the clergy. This was reversed two years later and overturned again in 1873.[9] Later in the 1870s, the Puerto Rican church's property – estimated at 400,000 pesos – was seized by the crown and used to compensate slaveholders for the abolition of slavery in 1873.[10] Part of the Catholic clergy opposed abolition. A Puerto Rican elected to the Spanish Cortes (parliament) in 1869, the Franciscan Juan Antonio Puig y Monserrat, argued against abolition, while the island's liberal representatives argued in favour. Some members of the clergy themselves owned slaves.[11] Puig y Monserrat's conservative views helped him in 1875 become bishop of San Juan, a post he would occupy for nearly twenty years.[12]

The church's social hegemony was challenged on other fronts as well. Civil marriage, recognized in Spain briefly in the early 1870s, was allowed in Puerto Rico in the 1880s.[13] At the end of the century, under US rule, divorce was permitted, and even priests could marry.[14] Earlier, in 1875, the governor, General Sanz y Posse, asked municipalities to establish cemeteries outside the Catholic cemetery "for those persons who would die outside the Catholic faith." The population already counted some Protestants and Freemasons; a decade later the curate of San Germán refused to bury in the Catholic cemetery a man reputed to be a Freemason.[15]

Puerto Rican clerics could be touchy about public challenges to their privileges and authority. In 1871, the parish priest of Vega Baja denounced to the local government a man who had not knelt when a Corpus Christi procession passed in front of his house.[16] The man, Manuel Fernández Juncos, was a poet and journalist who later founded many newspapers of a progressive bent and became a prominent politician as well as a Freemason.[17] The priest was probably aware of his political ideas and sought to harass him. In 1887, a parish priest complained to the bishop that some people did not remove their hats when he passed by them, and that some stores did not close during religious processions or during Sunday Mass.[18]

These were but incidents in the mounting challenges the rise of liberal thought was bringing the church. Liberals claimed to be governed by reason and science. They believed in human rights for everyone and claimed the right to free expression. Liberal principles were the foundation for Betances's "Ten Commandments of Free Men," which included, besides freedom of religion and the abolition of slavery, freedom of speech, of the press, and of commerce, the right of assembly, and the inviolability of citizens.[19]

Publications of all sorts were proliferating, many of them espousing liberal principles. Between 1870 and 1874, 45 periodicals were launched, and 410 between 1880 and 1898; 318 books were published between 1874 and 1898. All these publications faced the continuing imposition of censorship. Reading rooms, where this new printed material could be consulted, appeared across the island.[20]

The Catholic hierarchy resisted liberalism with its own printed medium. In 1859, it launched the *Boletín Eclesiástico*, the church's combative voice. It not only disseminated news and views from the local hierarchy and from Rome, but also challenged freedom of the press, the rationalism of Enlightenment thought, Freemasonry, the labour movement, and socialism. It defended censure, absolute monarchy, the Spanish colonial regime, and the temporal power of the pope. Locally, it fought against civil marriage and the burial of non-Catholics in parish cemeteries.[21]

WEAKNESS OF THE SPANISH CLERGY

Nineteenth-century Spain recognized the weakness of Catholic priests in its remaining colonies. In the 1860s, it allowed Augustinian, Dominican, Franciscan, and Jesuit orders "to establish a small number of houses to train priests for Cuba, Puerto Rico, and the Philippines."[22] In the next decade, the bishop of Puerto Rico suggested to the local governor mandating Jesuits to carry out Christianizing missions in rural areas[23] since Spanish secular clerics lacked formal training in pastoral work. As a specialist on the Spanish church put it, many parish priests "resorted to the time-honoured custom of lifting their discourses from printed collections of sermons, a device that often left simple rural congregations confounded before 'the pompous language' employed. Another cleric with years of pastoral experience in southern Spain believed ... that some parish priests avoided giving many sermons on the grounds that it was too exhausting for their parishioners to hear the same sermon over again."[24] Priests used the catechism to teach the rudiments of the faith by rote, but most of the ones in use, even as late as 1900, had been written in the seventeenth century.[25]

Priests were not always good examples of adherence to the church's precepts. Priests with mistresses "had formed part of the social history of the Spanish clergy for centuries despite repeated ecclesiastical censure." Politically, regular clergymen in Spain were reputed to constitute a "'redoubt of integrism,' by which is meant a fundamental opposition to the secular and, such as it was, pluralistic society created by liberalism."[26]

POPULAR RELIGIOUS PRACTICES IN SPAIN

Late-century Spain continued to witness manifestations of popular religion, particularly in small towns and rural areas. These devotions, of course, were practised in Puerto Rico as well, reinforced with the arrival of *peninsulares*. Belief in magic, witchcraft, the power of the dead, holy patrons, and the supernatural virtues of local shrines "served as a vehicle for the expression of local patterns of sociability." Even in cities, traditional community ceremonies, such as Holy Week processions, continued, taking on the secular character of tourist attractions.[27]

Attendance at Sunday Mass and the taking of the Eucharist became more prevalent in Spain during this period. Veneration of the exposed Eucharist included benedictions and adoration, and brotherhoods were dedicated to the cult of the Eucharist, including that of the Nocturnal Adoration.[28]

Devotion to the Virgin Mary expanded and took many local forms: the Immaculate Virgin, the Virgin of the *dolores* (pains), of *soledad* (solitude), *del pilar* (of the pillar), of *merced* (mercy), and *del Carmen* (of Mount Carmel). The rosary was recited three times daily, particularly during the month before Christmas. May became the month of Mary, borrowing an Italian custom. Young women could join the Daughters of Mary, and there were brotherhoods dedicated to the Heart of Mary.[29]

THE FIRST PROTESTANT INSTITUTIONS

Protestantism reached Puerto Rico a few decades before the American conquest. In 1867, the Catholic *Boletín Eclesiástico* published a priestly denunciation of Protestant publications arriving from the United States. Protestantism it derided as lacking in symbols, its articles of faith so changeable as to be meaningless.[30] Some Protestants, whether visiting or resident, lived in Ponce and the island of Vieques before their religion was officially allowed on the island.[31] After Spain granted liberty of religion within its empire in 1869, Protestant churches began to appear, notably the Anglican church in Ponce. Its first church building was open to "the public" in 1874; it served the English-speaking mercantile community in the island's main trading centre.[32] The minister began spreading Protestant notions in the countryside, largely devoid of Catholic clergy. He distributed leaflets and Protestant Bibles translated into Spanish,[33] even though the 1860 census showed less than 10 per cent of the population literate.[34]

Lay Protestants also attempted to convert people. In Aguadilla in 1880, a Protestant landowner named Hellinger converted one of his friends, giving rise to a group named Los Bíblicos, who would later find common ground with newly arrived Presbyterians.[35]

FREEMASONS, SPIRITISTS, AND *ESPIRITISTAS*

The gradual liberalization of the Spanish state was extending to Puerto Rican society. Freemasons of Spanish obedience (there were also Freemasons of French obedience in the west-coast town of Mayagüez, including a priest, from 1821 to 1841),[36] organized lodges throughout the island in the 1880s and 1890s.[37]

Masonic lodges were associations dedicated to personal development, ethical behaviour, social reform, ideas of freedom, tolerance, and acceptance of all human beings, progress, enlightenment, charitable works, and of course mutual financial and social assistance.[38] They believed in a Superior Being as the "Grand Architect of the Universe" but eschewed further religious dogma. They formed part of the wider liberal challenge to the established religious and political order in Spain and on the island.[39] Masonic Lodges grew rapidly in numbers, so that in 1884 they were able to form the Provincial Grand Lodge of Puerto Rico, which became the Sovereign Grand Lodge of Puerto Rico the following year.[40]

Some Freemasons arrived from Spain as civil servants and would make up the majority of the Puerto Rican cabinet when Spain granted autonomy in 1897.[41] Eighty-six lodges were established between 1871 and 1900, and 1,832 members have been identified: more than two-thirds were native-born, most of the rest coming from Spain. But three-quarters of lodges did not last five years. Freemasons came from all classes of society, but mainly from the upper tiers of industrialists, civil servants, and merchants. They welcomed people from different countries, regardless of race or colour.[42]

Freemasons were occasionally the target of the local government, such as those members of the San Germán lodge who were arrested in 1874 for being Freemasons; they were released two years later by the Spanish government at the urging of the British prime minister. Opponents of the Freemasons sought to tar them as separatists,[43] perhaps not without cause, at least for the earlier lodges in San Juan. In 1865, the *Boletín Eclesiástico* angrily claimed Freemasonry was an anti-Catholic secret society that tolerated barbaric customs such as cannibalism. In 1883, a Ponce Freemason was condemned to six months in jail for having published an article considered offensive to the church. Freemasons could be barred from the Catholic sacraments and burial in consecrated ground. They were blamed for the 1899 San Ciriaco hurricane that devastated the island.[44]

Freemasons published a newspaper in Ponce in 1880[45] and another one in Mayagüez, *La Adelphia*, which was condemned by the state and suspended publication in 1884.[46] These were part of the efflorescence of periodical publications from the 1870s on.[47] Freemasons also helped create schools and libraries.[48] Antagonism persisted from the Catholic church and local authorities – in 1893, for example, the curate of Yacuboa, on the southeastern edge of the island, refused baptism to children of Freemasons, while in Guayama, in the south, civil authorities ordered the closing of a play because the director was a Freemason.[49] Freemasonry would continue to grow after 1900 and would boast about 3,000 members between 1900 and 1930. Lodges gradually changed their allegiance from Spain to the United States.[50]

Challenges to Catholic orthodoxy arose also from adherents of spiritism, an intellectual movement inspired by a Frenchman under the nom de plume Allan Kardec, who sought to bridge "*science, philosophy, and religion* into a new way of looking at life, the afterlife, and the world around us – both visible and invisible."[51] It was one of the many spiritual movements of the mid-nineteenth century that featured "*séances*" of speaking spirits, table-turning, and mediums through whom one communicated with the unseen world. Kardec was a polymath who had an interest in phrenology, magnetism, clairvoyance, and hypnosis; he learned of the ties between the seen and the unseen worlds through two young female mediums of his acquaintance.[52] In 1857, he published *Le livre des esprits*, which put on paper what the spirits had conveyed to him about the links between science and religion, knowledge which, he noted in the preface to the revised edition, had been communicated to others before him, notably by "the most eminent thinkers of ancient and modern times."[53]

Kardec's ideas spread swiftly to Spain – where his books were burned by order of the bishop of Barcelona in 1861 – and to Latin America.[54] Already in San Juan in 1856, "*séances*" were the rage among men of judgment and imagination, noted a popular magazine. Three years later, the *Boletín Eclesiástico* condemned spiritism along with Protestantism and Freemasonry.[55] Secret groups of spiritists formed in Mayagüez (a centre of enlightenment, it seems) in the early 1870s – in 1871 according to some, in

1875 according to another source – and bookstores in San Juan sold Kardec's works in 1873.[56] The previous year, a Puerto Rican deputy to the Spanish Cortes sought to replace metaphysics with spiritism in the secondary-school curriculum.[57]

The early adherents to Kardec's philosophy in Puerto Rico, as in Cuba, were from the literate middle class[58] that also turned to Freemasonry and to anti-clericalism. They challenged the church's efforts to end common-law unions as an intrusion of religion into civil affairs.[59] Politically, they tended also to oppose local authorities' repression of ideas.[60]

Despite the church's opposition to "heterodoxy" – it proscribed Kardec's books in 1874[61] – the 1880s saw spiritism burgeon in the island's press and in the formation of spiritist societies.[62] In 1888, a delegation from Mayagüez took part in the first international congress of spiritists in Barcelona. Puerto Rican spiritists promoted social and political reforms and established hospitals, hospices, and medical clinics, while some advocated independence.[63]

This middle-class, intellectual form of spiritism, with its belief in the alliance between faith and science, was amalgamated by the "urban and rural lower classes" with native healing systems to give rise to *espiritismo*, a widespread form of syncretism.[64] This form of spiritism drew also from popular Catholic rituals that relied on direct contact with saints and guardian angels to obtain favours,[65] forming a "community healing system."[66]

Historians have found in the Puerto Rican press of this era some manifestations of this Indigenous spiritism. In October 1880, a group of persons "of different sexes, colour, condition, and age" – this mixture by itself a challenge to the established order – carried out an "unspeakable parody of a procession" in Río Piedras, a suburb of San Juan, for which they were arrested, since this was not their first offence, noted the conservative *Boletín Mercantil*. Their leader claimed the group had been invested with a sacred apostolate by St Augustine.[67] Four years later, *El Imparcial*, a Mayagüez newspaper, reported that eight persons were arrested in Río Grande, east of San Juan, for making curious gestures and calling themselves "*espiritistas*"; the paper commented sarcastically that if this was indeed a crime, then the crime rate would soar.[68]

The popularity of both forms of spiritism, "scientific" and "Indigenous," compelled the Catholic hierarchy to redouble its efforts to preserve its hegemony. It mobilized its parish priests, preachers, writers, periodicals, as well as the more notable among its flock, to denounce heterodoxy, but it failed in driving out spiritism from the island.[69]

Political and constitutional changes in Spain had lessened somewhat the Catholic church's official status and put it on the ideological defensive. Its clerical forces remained ill-equipped to improve popular religious practices. Nevertheless, formal popular devotions became more widespread, and this pattern could be observed in Puerto Rico as well.

On the island, religious heterodoxy became more visible.[70] Besides many intellectuals' anti-clericalism,[71] the burgeoning of Freemasonry and of the various forms of spiritism offered alternative communities of the soul. Protestantism broadened this offer, though attracting adherents mainly from the merchants of Ponce and immigrant workers in Vieques.

The US invasion of 1898 would accelerate this trend towards religious pluralism on the island.

6

~

American Dominion, 1898–1930

Puerto Rico's abrupt change of empire in 1898 transformed the status of the island's Catholic faith. The church lost its state protection and its meagre financial support. Its links with its flock continued to weaken, as Spanish-born priests returned home, forcing recruitment of American candidates, even more culturally removed from their parishioners than the ones they replaced. The church's role in public education ended, and it had to establish Catholic schools to retain some influence in educating the young. In the field, its weak presence created a void that lay preachers, both male and female, undertook to fill, with some success.

THE US GOAL OF PROTESTANT CONVERSION

With its conquest of Puerto Rico, the United States had to govern a people culturally alien to it both in language and in religion. The US government appointed a special commissioner, Henry K. Carroll, to report on the "civil, industrial, financial, and social conditions" on the island. After he toured Puerto Rico and met with inhabitants of all classes, Carroll's voluminous report of 6 October 1899 recommended that the "Constitution and laws of the United States be extended to Porto [*sic*] Rico" and that "congregations using church edifices for public worship shall not be disturbed in the use thereof until the question of legal title thereto is settled." The application of the US constitution and laws would be welcome, he argued, as "people seem to be entirely in accord with the American principle of separation of church and state, and complete religious liberty."[1] The Treaty of Paris that ended the Spanish-American war in 1898 guaranteed freedom of religion to inhabitants of the ceded territories.[2]

The principle of liberty of religion did not extend to education. Carroll, who was a Methodist minister, recommended that "the governor-general and legislature of Porto Rico be required to make provision for universal and obligatory education in a system of free public schools, in which the English language shall be taught."[3] Language was to be the instrument of assimilation into US culture, and removing the teaching of Catholicism in public schools would facilitate Protestant missionary work. The US military administration, which ruled the island for two years and retained influence over its affairs until the 1930s,[4] supported the drive to Protestantism. Indeed, the mandate given to Victor S. Clark as head (1899–1900) of the Insular Board of Education for Puerto Rico[5] stated that "an education which proposes a change to the native tongue implies a change of religion and the complete transformation of the body of traditions of the people."[6] The end of Spanish rule terminated state salaries to Catholic priests, leaving the remaining incumbents to rely on parishioners.[7] Residents feared that, as Spain had imposed Catholicism, the United States would impose Protestantism, according to the island's bishop, James Hubert Blenk, in his 1905 *Report on the Diocese of Puerto Rico* to the Vatican.[8] The institution of civil marriage and divorce during military rule could begin this process. Some members of the liberal elite welcomed the chance to constrain the church by proposing in the legislature, in 1900, suppression of the Sisters of Charity, prohibition of processions and other religious activities in public spaces, and transfer to the government of the registers of baptisms, marriages, and deaths kept by parish priests. The proposal did not become law.[9]

THE CHURCH'S NEW SITUATION

The tensions between liberals and orthodox Catholics brewing since the 1870s came to the fore in the months following the conquest. In October 1898 in Juana Díaz, on the south side of the island, the Sisters of Charity, who ran a school for poor children, asked the city to pay their wages, not

received since June. The city refused, while it supported a proposal to open
a lay high school. In San Germán, the parish priests, who were Spanish, fled
the city for fear the arrival of the Americans would embolden the locals
who hated Spaniards, especially priests. Elsewhere, secular priests replaced
the Spanish-born regular clerics who had returned to Spain. When Bishop
Blenk arrived in 1899, he noted that thirty-four parishes lacked priests,
while many clerics who remained did not have appropriate training or ad-
equate personal discipline. At least one priest and over one hundred male
and female religious made a declaration of Spanish nationality before
municipal authorities, in order to be able to return to Spain. Three of the
four Catholic orders left before 1901, now unsupported by the Spanish state.
Most female religious orders, however, remained, boasting a greater proportion of island-born members; their charitable work was appreciated
and supported locally.[10]

The Church's Ambiguous Reaction to US Dominion

In his study of the Catholic church and Americanization until 1930, Samuel
Silva Gotay argues that the church was involved in the process, though not
always deliberately. Its top hierarchy was American: every bishop from 1899
to 1960, except for one from 1921 to 1925, was American. The hierarchy pur-
sued the same process of Americanization that was reshaping the Catholic
church on the mainland. During the Spanish-American War, US Catholic
bishops proclaimed their allegiance to the United States, insisting that "no
true American Catholic should dare support the Spanish side because Spain
was a Catholic country."[11] The US hierarchy engaged in what Stevens Arroyo
has labelled "pious colonialism," or colonialism through Catholic institutions.[12] After 1900, the church established a network of private Catholic
schools on the island to teach English and US culture, but it neglected to
cultivate native vocations. Among Catholic clerics, though not among leaders, there was strong support for autonomy or independence, which equated
being Puerto Rican with being Catholic.[13] We may thus observe some ambiguity about the US dominion within the ranks of the island's church.

The laity also resisted the new order and developed a countervailing emphasis on *hispanidad* (Hispanic identity). An *Asociación de Católicos* was
formed in 1899 in Ponce, under the inspiration of the Paulist fathers, who
had charge of the city's Virgen de Guadalupe parish. The association

launched its own periodical, *El Ideal Católico*, in August 1899. It soon spread to San Juan and other localities. The association was made up largely of professionals – doctors and lawyers – both Puerto Rican- and Spanish-born. In 1900, *El Ideal Católico* decried the presence of American Protestant ministers and the construction of Protestant churches all over the island as American money flooded in after the conquest; without these resources, it claimed, there would be no Protestantism on the island.[14]

Ambiguity could surface in the same person at different times. In 1899, *El Ideal Católico* reported that, on the day of his meeting with the US president, recently appointed Bishop Blenk stated that "soon the Americanization of the island would become a fact." Yet some years later, in 1913, Blenk, by then bishop of New Orleans, wrote to an independentist friend in Puerto Rico to congratulate him on his efforts to achieve his ideals and wished him God's help in pursuing his "beautiful and justified ideals." When this letter became public knowledge, Bishop Jones, who succeeded Bishop Blenk in 1907, reaffirmed, through his diocesan publication, the church's non-political stance, while condemning the independence movement as "ill-advised." In the same year, during the four hundredth anniversary of the foundation of the diocese and the transfer of the remains of Spanish explorer and *conquistador* Ponce de León to San Juan, many speeches were filled with declarations of hispanidad, leading Archbishop John Farley of New York, who had attended the event, to stand against Puerto Rican independence in an interview with the *New York Times*.[15]

Defence of the faith and defence of the nation and of hispanidad were particularly salient in Ponce, where liberals controlled the local administration and were representatives to the island's Chamber of Delegates.[16] But the Catholic hierarchy did not tolerate overt political opposition. Thus, in Vieques, when the local parish priest took up the fight against liberals, atheists, and opponents of religion by attempting to create a political party, he was rebuked by his bishop.[17]

The Rise of Catholic Personnel

There were 137 parish priests in Puerto Rico at the US conquest. Of the eighty-six parishes, only thirty-four had a curate.[18] The newly arriving Bishop Blenk set out to recruit priests from regular orders abroad. These men, of whom he was one, were better trained and led a more austere life than secular clergy. Augustinian fathers arrived from Spain in 1901, American Redemptorists in 1902, Dominicans from Holland in 1904, and Capuchins from Spain in 1905. The last were replaced in 1929 by Capuchins from the United States.[19] In Mayagüez, the Redemptorists restored the parish church and equipped two schools as well as convents and chapels. The American Catholic Church Extension Society helped to finance missionary work and the local church, as it sought to slow the growth of Protestantism.[20] All the teaching orders recruited by Bishop Blenk came from the United States.[21]

Bishop Jones continued relying on foreign regular orders. By 1920, he had assigned eleven parishes to regular clerics, including parishes in San Juan, in Río Piedras, Santurce, and Guaynabo, three suburbs of the capital, and in Caguas, about thirty kilometres (twenty miles) south of San Juan. The Dominicans were assigned the parishes of Yauco, Guánica, on the south side of the island, and Isabela, Cataño, and Palo Seco, on the north side. In 1920, Bishop Jones assigned the parishes of the islands of Culebra and Vieques to Carmelite Fathers. In all, foreign regular orders ministered to a third of the island's parishes. By 1930, there were nineteen religious orders in Puerto Rico, all from abroad: thirteen from the United States, five from Spain, and one from Holland.[22]

The bishops' reliance on foreign clergy for Puerto Rico, like Spain's use of metropolitan rather than local clergy there, soon drew criticism. In August 1909, the newspaper *La Democracia* accused the church of having put regular clergymen from the United States in the island's better parishes. This group was "totally foreign" and diminished the role of the island-born, "to whom belongs by rights the spiritual direction" of Puerto Ricans.[23]

The Sacred Heart nuns were the first US female missionaries invited by Archbishop Blenk. They arrived in San Juan in 1902. They looked after deaf children in San Juan, then in Cayey, south of Caguas, in Aguadilla, and in the Santurce suburb of San Juan. They visited from house to house and from hovel to hovel, getting people to receive the sacraments and confirmation on the bishop's visit.[24]

Six Dominican nuns from Amityville, NY, arrived in 1910 at the bishop's request. They established schools in Comerío and Yauco on the island's south side, in San Juan and in Cataño, across the bay from the capital.[25] By 1917, there were eleven female religious institutions in San Juan, five each in Mayagüez and in Ponce, two each in Arecibo, Río Piedras, San Germán, and Yauco, and one each in Caguas, Manatí, on the island's north side, and Vega Baja.[26] The Puerto Rican synod of 1917 reported 308 female religious and thirty-five males.[27] The Sisters of St Joseph, from New York, arrived in 1930. They opened a school in San Juan, travelled with their own car to visit rural areas, established a dispensary for children in Ponce, and performed numerous baptisms.[28]

As under Spanish rule, so in 1925: the majority of Catholic priests were of foreign origin; only twelve of the more than 150 priests were Puerto Ricans.[29] This Catholic clergy could not be as close to the people as would be their native-born Protestant counterparts.

RELIGION AND EDUCATION

For Catholics as for Protestants, primary and secondary denominational schools were the main channel for delivering religious instruction. For the first time, the Catholic church was excluded from public schools run by the island's new Department of Education, which would henceforth propel Protestant values. In a joint letter to the US war secretary in September 1899, Archbishop Chapelle of New Orleans, the apostolic delegate to Puerto Rico, and the island's new bishop, James Hubert Blenk, opposed the presence of schoolteachers from the United States. The church fought in vain against the removal of religious instruction from public schools. *El Ideal Católico* of May 1901 complained that it was a veritable anomaly that Puerto Rican Catholic taxpayers paid for public schools while school regulations were written and enforced by Protestant employees. Catholics were aware that Protestant missionaries were the "most arduous defenders" of public education. Protestant support for the system would continue well into the twentieth century. In 1907, *El Ideal Católico* reaffirmed the prohibition against Catholic parents sending their children to public schools.[30]

From 1898 to 1917, public schools taught in English, except for Spanish instruction. This was a failure, as a report noted in 1926. "General advancement was being severely handicapped" while "progress in spoken English was not as satisfactory as had been expected."[31]

The solution chosen was to create private Catholic schools. Three of the female religious orders Bishop Jones imported to establish schools did their teaching in English. Local authorities required this. These orders did not aim to "Americanize" students, but their members found it difficult to learn Spanish and to adapt to the local culture. Parish schools created to fight the public system's Protestant influence and proselytism ended up "in a sense less of an Americanizing influence than the public-school system," argues one scholar.[32]

But not by much. Private Catholic schools had both social-class and cultural features. By 1917, when the first Catholic synod under American rule gathered, there were twenty-four new Catholic private schools, the majority established by American congregations, resulting in Catholic education for wealthier people, and an environment that in effect Americanized their children. Most Catholic schools taught in English in the later grades, including religious instruction.[33]

This adhered to the policy for public schools, which introduced English-only instruction in the primary grades. In 1922, the new commissioner of education, Juan B. Huyke, a Puerto Rican Protestant and member of the annexationist Union Party, decreed that English would be the language of instruction starting in the fourth grade, a year earlier than before. Speaking Spanish in the later grades was prohibited. The commissioner had sent 427 students to the United States to learn the English language and American customs so that they would introduce these to the island.[34] Still, in the early 1920s there were fewer than one hundred teachers from the mainland, and 1,900 Puerto Rican teachers.[35]

In the 1930s, the bishop of Ponce, Aloysius Joseph Willinger, continued the fight for Catholic education and for religious instruction in public schools, reminding parents that their children were obligated to attend Catholic schools.[36]

FORMAL AND INFORMAL RELIGIOUS PRACTICES

During the 1900s and 1910s, Catholic religious orders the world over underwent greater centralization and the Vatican exercised tighter oversight, so that religious practices among the regular orders in Puerto Rico came to resemble those followed in New York, Paris, or Mexico City.[37] But the tension persisted between what the hierarchy deemed proper and what the laity practised. The Puerto Rican synod of 1917 declared that *ex votos* such as picture frames or similar objects left in churches as thanks for avoiding danger or regaining health represented "something false, indecorous or superstitious" and needed to be removed.[38]

Yet the Catholic hierarchy mobilized traditionally popular pilgrimages to Hormigueros, on the south-west side of the island, to honour the Virgin of Monserrate. Bishop Blenk organized a great celebration in Hormigueros for the fiftieth anniversary of the proclamation of the dogma of the Immaculate Conception in 1904. This religious ritual was seized upon by a local priest, who wrote in *El Ideal Católico* to urge readers to go to Hormigueros "for God and country," turning the pilgrimage into a nationalist symbol.[39]

Popular devotion to the Virgin Mary was reinforced in 1917 when Redemptorist Fathers convinced the synod to promote the cult of the Virgin of Perpetual Help.[40]

THE TENUOUS LINK BETWEEN
CHURCH AND PEOPLE

Church and people remained physically distant between 1898 and 1930. In 1899, a Protestant missionary noted "with some amazement" that there were no church buildings in rural areas. By the later 1940s, nearly two in five rural families lived more than five kilometres (three miles) from a church.[41]

Some Puerto Ricans maintained more than physical distance from the church. In 1900, an anti-clerical feminist published a tirade against the church in a Mayagüez periodical, criticizing the church's economic power, papal infallibility, and compulsory priestly celibacy. In response, the *Ideal Católico* accused the author of being inspired by Satan and denied her the right to take part in public debate because such forums were reserved to men.[42] In 1901, Cayetano Coll y Toste, a liberal member of the cabinet and of the Chamber of Delegates who would become the island's official historian, declared during a discussion in the chamber that he was not a Catholic, which earned him a reprimand from the *Boletín Eclesiástico*. The same year, a resident of Utuado wrote to the newspapers to have the ringing of church bells prohibited. In Aguadilla, some residents complained that the church required young people to attend the procession in honour of the parish's patron saint, St Charles Borromeo, instead of school; the residents asked the attorney general to prohibit the procession, which he refused to do. Between 1904–5 and 1912, 179 marriages were recorded in the island's civil register, sixty-nine of them civil and thirty-seven Protestant, leaving Catholic unions at seventy-three, or less than 40 per cent.[43]

RISE AND DECLINE OF SPIRITISM

As had happened in the 1880s and 1890s, many Puerto Ricans continued to look beyond the formal church to fathom their place in the world. Spiritism provided some of this understanding. Spiritists believed in God as a supreme intelligence of infinite size, in the eternal life of the soul, in reincarnation, in the virtue of doing good and in the price to pay for bad behaviour, in Christ as an immensely evolved spirit, but not in the devil or in Hell, as these would negate the supreme goodness of God.[44] In 1903, some spiritist leaders set up the Spiritist Federation of Puerto Rico to better organize the island's groups of adherents, who proposed programs of social action, such as abolition of the death penalty. Spiritists organized their own institutions of social welfare, opening health clinics and hospitals for the poor, which helped spread their influence.[45]

Spiritists believed men and women should be equal in the family. In 1899, some female spiritists launched *El Iris de Paz*, a periodical devoted to "social feminism" that lasted until 1912. It advocated marriage as a union based on love and spiritual and intellectual affinity. It criticized orthodox Catholic women for being submissive to the church's traditional views on the role of women. Women made up to a quarter of the delegates to the annual meetings of the Spiritist Federation of Puerto Rico. Their feminist positions brought them into open conflict with traditional Catholic stances espoused by *El Ideal Católico*, which announced in 1901 that the hierarchy had forbidden the reading of *El Iris de Paz*.[46]

Spiritism spread to rural areas, where its rituals had more appeal than its "scientific" character. It became a complement to folk Catholicism, which viewed nature as endowed with supernatural powers to be channelled for everyday life. It added to the cult of the saints, to the belief in waters with magical powers to cure sickness, prevent hunger, and avoid death.[47]

The most visible and publicized instance of popular faith healing associated with spiritism was Julia Vázquez of San Lorenzo, nicknamed The
Samaritan (for the New Testament figure who saved a stranger), who at-
tained media fame for healing with water. Thousands of pilgrims, "mostly
latter-day jíbaros (subsistence farmers)," travelled to San Lorenzo in the
spring and summer of 1922 to be healed by The Samaritan.[48]

Julia Vázquez was "a poor woman of colour" who drew thick crowds on
Thursdays and Fridays, "the days that Vázquez's spirit guides had designated for her public work." She gave her patients *agua fluidizada*, a practice
well known to spiritists everywhere and familiar to Puerto Ricans at least
since the 1890s. The Samaritan took spring water and "magnetized" it during her communications with her spirit guide. Followers took the water
home and used it much as Catholics used holy water, by drinking it or ap-
plying it to their body. The Samaritan did not only cure; her work was "also
an intervention in favour of moral regeneration and spiritual advancement
for society."[49]

Her story filled the newspapers and was made into a blockbuster movie
that premièred in San Juan in July 1922 to a sold-out audience. "The media's
and the public's interests owed a good deal to the intervention of the group
of spiritists that included several federation leaders who orchestrated a skill-
ful propaganda campaign in *La Samaritana*'s favour"[50] (see figure 6.1).

Spiritism in the 1930s lost ground to the growing awareness of natural
and social sciences with clinical and social-welfare applications. "However,
the substance of the movement persisted in the highly syncretic practices
of the folk."[51]

PROPHETS FROM THE PUEBLOS

These "syncretic practices" were encouraged and strengthened with the
spontaneous appearance, soon after the American conquest, of popular lay
preachers in the rural areas of the island. The best-known of these were the
Cheos brothers. Some scholars have attributed their rise to insecurities en-
gendered by the change of empire,[52] but this seems a bit facile, as there were
quite a few predecessors, some before 1898, whose reasons for their missions
remain obscure.[53]

LA ANIMADA ESCENA QUE TODAVIA SE CONTEMPLA EN LAS ALTURAS DE SAN LORENZO

Como nota curiosa y pintoresca traemos hoy a esta página una interesante fotografía que basta para dar una exacta idea del fanático fervor con que las muchedumbres acuden a las alturas de San Lorenzo, en pos del "agua maravillosa". Julia Vázquez, convertida por la exaltación popular en moderna "Samaritana", sigue, como podrá ver el lector, cautivando las multitudes que en automóviles, a caballo y a pie, marchan hipnotizadas tras del ansiado manantial que muchos juzgan, en su cándida ilusión, la mejor panacea salvadora...

Figure 6.1 The crowd in San Lorenzo. *Puerto Rico Ilustrado*, 2 September 1922.

The First Female Preachers

The first lay preacher to be mentioned by scholars studying this phenomenon was Sister Eudosia, a nineteen-year-old from Quebradillas, on the north-western edge of the island, who began preaching from her porch on 15 August 1898, two days after news of the US-Spanish armistice reached the island.[54] She preached until her death three years later, reciting the rosary and making prophecies. According to a clerical student of lay preachers, she laid the basis for the advent of the Cheos brothers by converting a farmer, Eusebio Quiles, to preach locally.[55]

A better-known predecessor to the Cheos brothers was Madre Elenita, from the San Lorenzo area, southeast of Caguas. She began preaching in 1899 in San Lorenzo, and then Caguas, Cayey, Arroyo, Patillas, Guayama, and Yacuboa, until her death in 1909 (see figure 6.2). She preached against common-law unions, immorality, and the lax Catholicism of the peasants. She warned them against the religion of the new political regime, drew

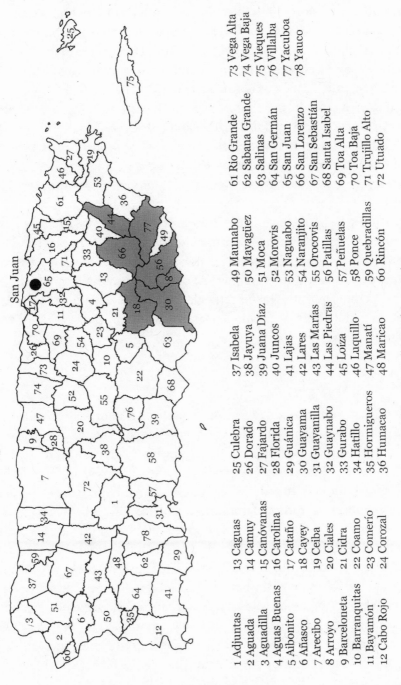

Figure 6.2 Madre Elenita's preaching territory, 1899–1909.

1 Adjuntas
2 Aguada
3 Aguadilla
4 Aguas Buenas
5 Aibonito
6 Añasco
7 Arecibo
8 Arroyo
9 Barceloneta
10 Barranquitas
11 Bayamón
12 Cabo Rojo

13 Caguas
14 Camuy
15 Canóvanas
16 Carolina
17 Cataño
18 Cayey
19 Ceiba
20 Ciales
21 Cidra
22 Coamo
23 Comerío
24 Corozal

25 Culebra
26 Dorado
27 Fajardo
28 Florida
29 Guánica
30 Guayama
31 Guayanilla
32 Guaynabo
33 Gurabo
34 Hatillo
35 Hormigueros
36 Humacao

37 Isabela
38 Jayuya
39 Juana Díaz
40 Juncos
41 Lajas
42 Lares
43 Las Marías
44 Las Piedras
45 Loíza
46 Luquillo
47 Manatí
48 Maricao

49 Maunabo
50 Mayagüez
51 Moca
52 Morovis
53 Naguabo
54 Naranjito
55 Orocovis
56 Patillas
57 Peñuelas
58 Ponce
59 Quebradillas
60 Rincón

61 Río Grande
62 Sabana Grande
63 Salinas
64 San Germán
65 San Juan
66 San Lorenzo
67 San Sebastián
68 Santa Isabel
69 Toa Alta
70 Toa Baja
71 Trujillo Alto
72 Utuado

73 Vega Alta
74 Vega Baja
75 Vieques
76 Villalba
77 Yacuboa
78 Yauco

them to the practice of the sacraments, prophesied, and made miracles, according to Catholic witnesses. She drew up to 5,000 followers from all areas of the island and was considered by some of them an incarnation of the Virgin Mary. She fostered the transformation of common-law unions in the region into formal Catholic marriages.[56]

In March 1901, during Sunday Mass in Quebradillas, a young woman named Juana interrupted the sermon and began preaching for the Archangel Gabriel. The parish priest stopped her, but she preached after Mass for more than one hour and a half to a large crowd. This was reported by *El Ideal Católico*.[57] She was said to be a shy person who spoke little in private but preached magnificently.[58] She later married a member of the Cheos.

As one scholar has remarked, "The role of the intermediaries, those who bridged the gaps between the church and Catholic practice, was gendered female at the outset." They were missionaries who "traveled to lead devotions in the countryside" and whose predications were reminiscent of those of the Capuchins. In their emphasis on the sacraments and their devotion to the Virgin, they complemented and extended the reach of the official church.[59]

The Cheos and Cheas

The Cheos Brothers (founders José de Los Santos Morales and José Rodríguez Medina shared the same first name, often rendered as "Cheo" in Puerto Rican vernacular) are the longest-lasting exemplar of lay preaching on the island. Their formal association, the Congregation of St John the Evangelist, was recognized by the Catholic church in 1927 and still exists today. Morales came from a farming family of Arecibo. He began preaching in January 1902, when he was only eighteen. Medina was five years older and commenced preaching in Utuado in 1903. They soon joined forces and spent several weeks preaching in Ponce. They drew crowds of sugar-cane workers who abandoned the harvest to hear them. The cane fields' owners complained to the police, who arrested the two preachers. Popular pressure led to their release on condition that they exhort their followers back to work and that they no longer preach during harvesting season.[60] This illustrates at once the strong appeal of the Cheos' preaching and their uneasy but usually compliant relationship with the authorities.

The Cheos led a "vast rural movement of poor laypersons, illiterate for the most part, who took into their own hands the predication of the Gospels to effect the conversion and the moral reconstruction of the rural areas and local communities in Puerto Rico, particularly where there had never, or seldom, been a priest."[61] They usually began their predication by invoking the protection of the saints, and denounced Protestantism, spiritism, superstition, Freemasonry, dancing, drinking, fornication, and adultery. They urged their followers to go to confession, attend Mass, and follow the Ten Commandments. They were fond of statues and crosses.[62] They set up their headquarters in Jayuya, in the mountainous interior of the island,[63] by building a chapel. They built chapels throughout the area to hold meetings and to preach, and to receive the sacraments from a priest on the feast day of the patron saint: by 1933 there were over thirty such chapels[64] (see figure 6.3).

The Catholic clergy at first viewed the Cheos preachers with some trepidation. In 1906, *El Ideal Católico* condemned them as being sent by the devil. A parish priest in Ponce wrote of them in 1909 that they were a bunch of *espiritistas*, crazies or fanatics who would preach for three to four hours to followers who mistook them for demi-gods and who obeyed them like docile little lambs. Still, he recognized that they had provoked an extraordinary increase in marriages and baptisms. In 1913, the Cheos sought Bishop Jones's blessing for their chapel in Jayuya, to be dedicated to St John the Evangelist and under the administration of nearby Utuado's Capuchin fathers. The bishop agreed to the blessing but declined to carry it out personally. In 1915, the Utuado parish priest reported favourably on the Cheos' positive influence on the peasants' behaviour.

In 1918, the Vatican officially blessed the Cheos movement and recognized its orthodoxy. The Cheos Roman Catholic Evangelistic Association of St John the Evangelist was formally established under canon law and put under the authority of the newly created bishopric of Ponce.[65]

The appearance of Protestant preachers in Puerto Rico after the American conquest has been said to have been one inspiration for the Cheos, who have been portrayed as a resistance movement against Americanization.[66] But the Cheos movement displayed notable elements of continuity with popular island religion. The "missionary" phenomenon, where "gifted priests preached intensively for a few days and then offered the sacraments

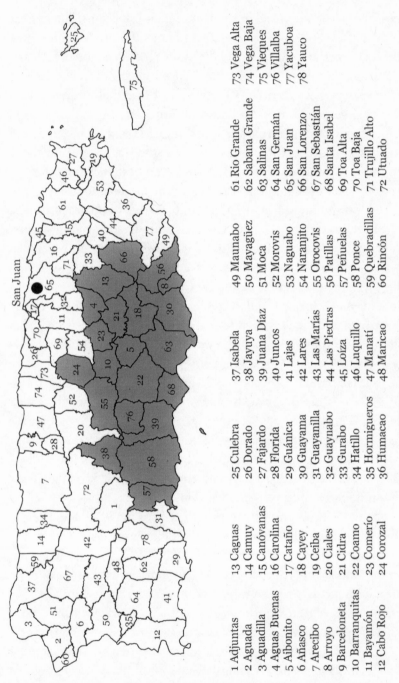

Figure 6.3 Approximate area of Cheos activity, 1902–1930s.

San Juan

1 Adjuntas	25 Culebra	49 Maunabo	73 Vega Alta
2 Aguada	26 Dorado	50 Mayagüez	74 Vega Baja
3 Aguadilla	27 Fajardo	51 Moca	75 Vieques
4 Aguas Buenas	28 Florida	52 Morovis	76 Villalba
5 Aibonito	29 Guánica	53 Naguabo	77 Yacuboa
6 Añasco	30 Guayama	54 Naranjito	78 Yauco
7 Arecibo	31 Guayanilla	55 Orocovis	
8 Arroyo	32 Guaynabo	56 Patillas	
9 Barceloneta	33 Gurabo	57 Peñuelas	
10 Barranquitas	34 Hatillo	58 Ponce	
11 Bayamón	35 Hormigueros	59 Quebradillas	
12 Cabo Rojo	36 Humacao	60 Rincón	
13 Caguas	37 Isabela	61 Río Grande	
14 Camuy	38 Jayuya	62 Sabana Grande	
15 Canóvanas	39 Juana Díaz	63 Salinas	
16 Carolina	40 Juncos	64 San Germán	
17 Cataño	41 Lajas	65 San Juan	
18 Cayey	42 Lares	66 San Lorenzo	
19 Ceiba	43 Las Marías	67 San Sebastián	
20 Ciales	44 Las Piedras	68 Santa Isabel	
21 Cidra	45 Loíza	69 Toa Alta	
22 Coamo	46 Luquillo	70 Toa Baja	
23 Comerío	47 Manatí	71 Trujillo Alto	
24 Corozal	48 Maricao	72 Utuado	

to those congregated at the designated site," dated from the second half of the nineteenth century.[67] Devotion to the saints, as Agosto Cintrón noted, was long ingrained in the island's popular religious practice.[68] The Cheos walked in the steps of previous lay preachers, many of them women, as we saw above, who had drawn large crowds. They drew on the same themes, urging their followers to keep away from spiritism and Freemasonry, as well as Protestantism, and exhorting them to lead a more moral life and frequent the sacraments.

The Cheos acknowledged the influence of Madre Elenita. One of their members moved to San Lorenzo to become acquainted with her. The first retreat organized by Morales was held on the land given to the Cheos by Madre Elenita on the Sacred Mountain, originally Montaña de la Santa[69] (i.e., Madre Elenita), near San Lorenzo, which site is still a Cheos centre. The Cheos welcomed female preachers – another major departure from Catholic tradition – if they remained obedient to the leadership.

Women were indeed prominent as preachers within the Cheos movement. José Morales's first wife, Micaela Reyes, preached in the local chapel and took care of visiting pilgrims, "particularly when her husband was away preaching elsewhere on the island."[70] They had married in 1907, before which she had been a "secular missionary." Maria Lamberty Orana was an independent lay preacher in Adjuntas, between Ponce and Arecibo, where she met the Cheos leaders; she would later marry Pedro Laboy Torres, who became the second president of the Cheos brothers. Juanita, the wife of one of José Morales's earliest collaborators in predication, Gregorio Rodríguez, also became a preacher; she had been inspired by Sister Eudosia.[71]

Eugenia Torres had a remarkable career. Known as Hermana Geña, she began preaching at fourteen after attending a predication by José Morales, and she preached in Ponce, Peñuelas, west of Ponce, San Lorenzo, Caguas, and nearby Cidra until her death in 1974. She was said to be beautiful, with gentle manners and admirable eloquence. When she married, the Cheos leadership ordered her to end her preaching. She left her husband and her children and moved to Ponce, where she worked at the hospice for the blind. When her husband died, she placed her children in an orphanage and took up preaching, "free again." She built a house, a chapel, and a building in which to conduct retreats in Cidra. Significantly, her resumption of preaching was allowed not only by José Morales, but by the bishop of San Juan, Edwin Vincent Byrne.[72]

Eugenia Torres told the story of a timid eight-year-old girl, Gumersinda Ríos, from Camuy, west of Arecibo, whose father brought her to a Cheos meeting in Jayuya and who began preaching standing on a table on which José Morales had set her because of her short height. Torres recalled that she heard from the child the explanation of the Holy Rosary and the panegyric of St Dominic de Guzmán, the thirteenth-century founder of the Dominican Order. Ríos was with the Cheos for three years, then fell ill and died.[73]

The female preachers associated with the Cheos had some competition from Protestant counterparts. In Mayagüez, a North American woman ran the Presbyterian Missionary School, which produced the female missionaries Esperanza Ruiz and Lolita Benavent.[74] The Protestant missionary effort in Puerto Rico soon grew into a large-scale enterprise.

The US conquest of Puerto Rico transformed the Catholic church's legal and social status on the island. The church lost the state's protection and financial support, ending its official presence in state education. The church lost many of its few priests and had to seek replacements mainly among the foreign Catholic clergy of the United States. The church reacted with some ambivalence to the new political order, some of its members accepting Americanization, others equating Catholicism with hispanidad and resisting cultural change.

The church's links with its laity remained thin. Popular religious practices, such as processions and pilgrimages, continued under its auspices. But it could not contain the rise of spiritism and other forms of faith healing. Its institutional weakness and its remoteness from parishioners outside the main centres prompted the rise of lay preachers, many of them women, who drew substantial followings as they attempted to resist new forms of religion and bring the common folk back to an orthodox practice of Catholicism.

7

~

Protestantism, 1898–1960

Besides losing official status and seeing many of its priests replaced by Americans, the Catholic church in Puerto Rico after 1898 faced a well-organized and -financed invasion by several US Protestant denominations intent on converting islanders to their faith and to American values. Protestant missionaries, educators, and health and social workers spread out around the island seeking sustained interaction with the inhabitants. Under the American principle of the separation of church and state, all Christian churches and other religions could now compete on an equal footing.

A TERRITORY DIVIDED: ARRIVAL OF THE HISTORICAL PROTESTANT DENOMINATIONS

Even before the Spanish-American war ended, representatives of the US "historical" Protestant denominations (Baptist, Congregational, Episcopal, Methodist, and Presbyterian) met in New York to apportion Puerto Rico among themselves. Protestant missionary groups met on 13 July 1898, nearly two weeks before US troops landed on the island. The following year, a map was drawn up to formalize the agreement among Baptists, the Christian

Alliance, the Church of Christ, Congregationalists, Disciples of Christ, Lutherans, Methodists, Presbyterians, and United Brethren. The Episcopalians rejected the zone system and ministered to the whole island (see figure 7.1).[1]

In 1905, a new map granted territory to Adventists, the Christian Alliance, Episcopalians, and Lutherans, allowing more than one denomination in twelve municipalities. The larger cities were open to all participating groups, and denominations that first began missionary work in municipalities with not more than 7,500 people could be exclusive there. These concords would be revised in the light of increasing population and urbanization (see figure 7.2).[2]

Protestant missionaries arrived with the American army. The US Protestant Episcopal Church set up a commission to study missionary work within the framework of a military chaplaincy and took over existing Episcopal churches in Ponce and Vieques. By the end of October 1898, a North American Baptist missionary to Mexico visited the island and began preaching in Spanish in Ponce, in Río Piedras, and elsewhere, to Catholic objections. Some months later arrived a US Baptist preacher. In the autumn of 1899, a young Lutheran pastor started to preach in San Juan: he gave English classes but needed a translator for sermons in Spanish. At about the same time Congregational teachers set up Protestant denominational schools. The Disciples of Christ sent a pastor to assess the situation; he was then appointed missionary to the island. The Methodists, as well, appointed missionaries, who began by preaching to Americans and later in Spanish to the locals. The Christian Alliance, the Christian Church of Jesus Christ, the Christian Church of the United States, the Methodists, the Seventh Day Adventists, and the United Brethren all did likewise.[3]

THE DEVELOPMENT OF
PUERTO RICAN PROTESTANTISM

Protestant missionaries had some immediate successes. They established schools so that children could learn to write and read the Bible, the foundation of Protestant preaching. They also engaged in social-welfare work, opening orphanages and hospitals for their flock. Protestant clergymen were aided

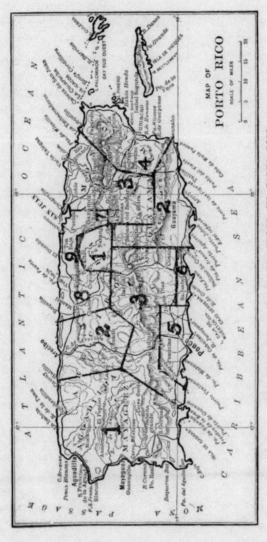

THE DIVISION OF MISSION FIELDS IN PORTO RICO

1, 1. Presbyterian (also San Juan)   4. Congregational   7. Lutheran
2, 2. Methodist   5. United Brethren   8. Christian Alliance
3, 3. Baptist   6. Christian Church 9. Church of Christ

Figure 7.1 Division of Mission Fields in Puerto Rico, 1899.

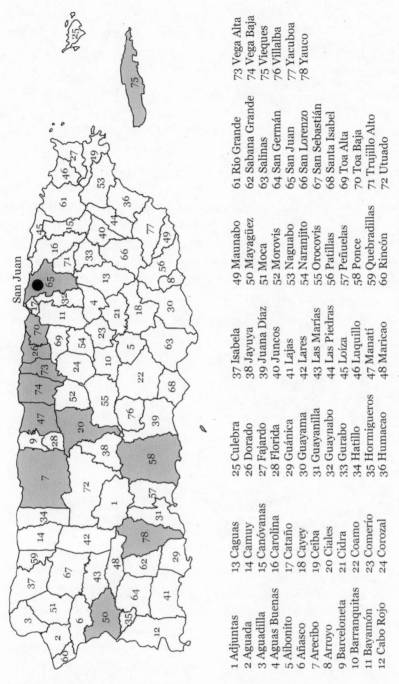

Figure 7.2 Municipalities with more than one active Protestant denomination, 1905.

1 Adjuntas
2 Aguada
3 Aguadilla
4 Aguas Buenas
5 Aibonito
6 Añasco
7 Arecibo
8 Arroyo
9 Barceloneta
10 Barranquitas
11 Bayamón
12 Cabo Rojo

13 Caguas
14 Camuy
15 Canóvanas
16 Carolina
17 Cataño
18 Cayey
19 Ceiba
20 Ciales
21 Cidra
22 Coamo
23 Comerío
24 Corozal

25 Culebra
26 Dorado
27 Fajardo
28 Florida
29 Guánica
30 Guayama
31 Guayanilla
32 Guaynabo
33 Gurabo
34 Hatillo
35 Hormigueros
36 Humacao

37 Isabela
38 Jayuya
39 Juana Díaz
40 Juncos
41 Lajas
42 Lares
43 Las Marías
44 Las Piedras
45 Loíza
46 Luquillo
47 Manatí
48 Maricao

49 Maunabo
50 Mayagüez
51 Moca
52 Morovis
53 Naguabo
54 Naranjito
55 Orocovis
56 Patillas
57 Peñuelas
58 Ponce
59 Quebradillas
60 Rincón

61 Río Grande
62 Sabana Grande
63 Salinas
64 San Germán
65 San Juan
66 San Lorenzo
67 San Sebastián
68 Santa Isabel
69 Toa Alta
70 Toa Baja
71 Trujillo Alto
72 Utuado

73 Vega Alta
74 Vega Baja
75 Vieques
76 Villalba
77 Yacuboa
78 Yauco

by their wives and children, a major difference with Catholic priests. Protestants introduced new institutions, values, and forms of religious practice, creating a religious and cultural shockwave across the island.[4]

These newcomers posed a highly visible challenge to the Catholic hierarchy. The first Episcopal church was named for John the Baptist (the island's patron saint, who gave his name to the capital) and was located across from the Catholic cathedral, next to the old Carmelite convent (today's El Convento hotel). That parish was soon headed by a bishop and boasted three parochial schools, for Americans in the capital and the Black population of the city's Puerta de Tierra neighbourhood. Episcopalians expanded to Ponce and Mayagüez. By 1912, they had four churches in the San Juan area, one in Mayagüez, four primary schools, and nine missionary centres in rural areas.[5]

The Lutherans formally arrived in San Juan in 1900. They established a Spanish-language parish, St Paul, and another parish and a school, in 1903, in Cataño. From there, they spread to Bayamón, Monacillo, a suburb of San Juan, Palo Seco, Toa Baja, Dorado, and other places. The Baptists, for their part, set up their first parish in Río Piedras, from which they expanded their preaching to Caguas, Ponce, Yauco, Guánica, Carolina, Trujillo Alto, Río Grande, Gurabo, Aguas Buenas, and Cidra (see map of Puerto Rico municipalities). In each of their parishes they appointed lay pastors to promote local membership. On the south side of the island in Ponce were the Baptist headquarters, where a seminary was established in 1906, and Baptist preachers travelled northward to preach in Coamo, Orocovis, and Barranquitas. By 1910, Baptists had set up forty-two churches in twenty-two municipalities, sixty-nine preaching centres, and fifty-six Sunday schools.[6]

The Congregationalists organized their first church in Fajardo in 1901. From there missionaries covered Luquillo, Naguabo, Ceiba, Humacao, Las Piedras, and Yabucoa, following the terms of the 1899 division. They focused on health services for Humacao and neighbouring towns.[7]

Methodists, too, arrived soon after the conquest. Their first churches were opened in the San Juan area in 1900 and in Arecibo two years later. The first Puerto Rican Methodist minister, Juan Vázquez of Arecibo, preached in Hatillo, Camuy, Jayuya, Utuado, in the southeast in Guayama, Arroyo, Maunabo, and Patillas, and on the islands of Vieques and Culebra.

Methodists also catered to English-speaking Protestants in the metropolitan area. By 1912, they had set up fourteen churches, a rest home for missionaries in Aibonito, and two orphanages. They focused on education and on night schooling for adults.[8]

Presbyterian missions were shaped by their US female missionaries. To achieve "an effective, rapid, symmetrical, and inclusive transformation of the intellectual, social, and moral character of Puerto Rico," they intended to emphasize their members' medical and educational work. Their territory was the west of the island: they set up their first parish in Mayagüez in 1902 and expanded to nearby municipalities such as Hormigueros, San Germán, Sabana Grande, and Cabo Rojo. They also set up parishes in Aguadilla and Santurce. Presbyterians founded a Polytechnic Institute (later the Universidad Interamericana de Puerto Rico), a hospital in Condado (now the Ashford Medical Center), and a nursing school.[9]

The Pentecostal church arrived in 1916. An evangelical denomination, it appealed to the poorer segments of society with its informal religious rites, its emphasis on possession by the Holy Spirit, and its adoption of the language and music of popular culture.[10] It was the precursor of many evangelical denominations that would later find numerous adherents on the island. Its social characteristics and its stress on preaching and on informality appealed to the sorts of people attracted to the many lay preachers exemplified by the Cheos brothers.

By and large, however, in the early twentieth century Protestantism increasingly appealed to merchants, professionals, and public servants, particularly in education.[11]

PROTESTANT BELIEFS

Whatever their denomination, Protestants shared some basic beliefs that contrasted sharply with Puerto Rico's Spanish-inflected Catholicism. They considered the Bible the only authoritative source on revelation, historically a rejection of the Catholic hierarchy's self-attributed authority in the matter. Their appropriation of the Bible was essential to their religion of personal conscience. The "*libre examen*" (unsupervised study) of the Bible, to support and understand one's beliefs, turned into a sort of individual right that came before everything else. For Protestants, Jesus Christ was the only head of the church and the only saviour and mediator between God and mankind by his sacrifice on the Cross. Salvation was possible only through faith in the loving and salutary power of Jesus Christ and never by church-administered sacraments, indulgences, or good works. All the faithful were part of the universal priesthood, and, as a consequence, life in common congregations was sacred.[12] These communities of the soul tended towards an egalitarian rather than a hierarchical structure.

Protestant preachers took this "good news" to all parts of the island, in the fields and in the mountains, on horseback and later by car. They tried to revisit the same places– perhaps the house of a recent convert – and established Bible schools. They became known as *la gente que predica* (the people who preach), in implicit contrast to Catholic clergymen, usually content to let their flock come to them in parish churches.[13]

EMPHASIS ON EDUCATION

The Bible's central role in Protestantism required education of the flock. Protestants became influential in public education as well as in denominational schools. Victor S. Clark, appointed in 1899 to head the Insular Board of Education, and director of public instruction 1900–02, was a Protestant pastor and educator.[14] The early leaders of the University of Puerto Rico, in the 1920s, were Protestant Puerto Ricans.[15] Until 1948, all secretaries of education, first Americans and then Puerto Ricans, were Protestants. "Furthermore, in many of the public schools the position of principal fell to Protestant ministers' wives."[16] Holidays honoured persons and events celebrated during US school holidays such as Washington's birthday (22 February), but excluded the most popular religious holiday on the island (Three Kings' Day, 6 January). Pupils nevertheless stayed away from school on that day, as Commissioner of Education Edwin G. Dexter recognized in a 1907 circular letter. "You are at liberty then to let it be generally known that that day will be taken by the teachers to fill out their registers and to arrange in the way that seems best for the general opening of the schools on the next day."[17]

In the 1900s and 1910s, Protestants created three kinds of schools. First, elementary and vocational schools were private denominational institutions to complement the public system. In 1910, there were thirty-five such, with 3,116 children, but only thirteen by 1915. The "general policy had been to establish such schools where there were no schools of the Department of Public Instruction."[18]

Second, Sunday schools, held after the weekly service, provided "recreation and entertainment in education and culture, religious reflection upon one's personal development that took place in groups so that their members examined their behaviour and the possibility of changing it. This contrasted with the teaching of the Catholic Church and the repetition of the Rosary at home and during the feast days of the religious calendar."[19]

Third, at summer retreats, "youth from various towns attended training in sport, recreational, and religious activities, producing not only generations of faithful with solid religious convictions grounded in the history of Protestantism ... and with a complete Biblical arsenal on which to base their faith, but also generations of young people strongly united by fraternal links." These efforts aimed consciously to create a "new man" – or woman – fashioned by the North American Protestant socio-economic, political, and cultural ethic.[20]

BEHAVIOURAL NORMS

Protestantism shaped adherents' daily life much more than Catholicism did its followers'. "Daily life of Protestants in these years was dominated by programs of their church: Biblical school on Sundays from 9 to 11 in the morning; meetings of committee or choir practice afterwards; visits to the sick in the afternoon; predication in the evening; prayers on Monday evenings, home devotions on Tuesdays and Wednesday evenings; choir practice Wednesdays or Thursdays; and men's, women's and youth group meetings on Friday evenings. Life within the congregation was a form of family life where one's problems were shared with all."[21] These activities drew strength from and strengthened the congregations that formed communities of the soul.

One pillar of that strength was the active role of women. From the outset, women took part in committees, commissions, and boards of directors;

they had voting rights within the congregation and in denominational conventions. They taught in Bible schools and directed prayers. They were numerous among the missionaries, doctors, teachers, social workers, and social reformers. It was stressed from the outset that Protestant Puerto Rican women attend school, and that classes be mixed.[22]

Protestants had no recourse such as Catholic confession to amend the flaws in their behaviour. As candidates for membership in a Baptist congregation, for instance, Puerto Ricans had to "relinquish their old religious practices, drinking, smoking, dancing, cockfighting, betting; they had to lead a strict marital and family life, they had to behave in an exemplary fashion at work, not engage in fighting, and take part in the life of the Church, including all its prayer meetings, its Bible classes, its youth, ladies' and men's groups, as well as visiting the sick and to speak of the Gospel to their relatives and neighbours." Belonging to – and remaining in – a Protestant denomination required submission to tight forms of social control. This was reinforced by an inclination to find a marital spouse within the religious community.[23]

GROWTH OF NUMBERS

With their schools, hospitals, medical clinics, orphanages, and social workers, Protestant missionaries to Puerto Rico confronted the poverty, illiteracy, ignorance, and ill health that plagued the island. Thus, they ministered to bodies as well as to souls in their efforts to "Americanize" and "modernize" mentalities. A good example was the Presbyterian Aguadilla Neighbourhood House, "which offered a school for poor children whose mothers worked, a dispensary, social work, a cooperative craft workshop for needlework, and evening classes for adults."[24]

The everyday evidence of Protestant care for the population translated into a rapid rise in membership. There were 8,000 adherents in "full communion" in 1905, 13,255 in 1910, and 13,250 in 1915. In 1905 already, there were ninety-one organized churches; in 1930, there were 199, with nearly 20,000 members.[25] Yet this was still a tiny minority of the total population, given as a million and a half in the US census.[26]

Protestants in 1930 belonged to ten denominations. While they had begun to work together in 1898 by dividing up the island's territory, they attempted to move to some form of inter-denominational structure by the 1910s. They merged some of their theological schools into the United Evangelical Seminary in 1916. By 1919 the Evangelical Seminary opened in Río Piedras, across the street from the campus of the University of Puerto Rico.[27]

THE GROWTH OF EVANGELICAL PROTESTANTISM, 1930–60

The social conventions at the heart of the Pentecostal churches that challenged "historical" Protestant churches for the faith of ordinary Puerto Ricans were more in tune with the "folk" practices of sociability and community self-help than were mainline Protestantism or authoritarian Catholicism. As Nélida Agosto Cintrón argues, in traditional society, particularly rural areas, orthodox Catholicism was perceived as mainly a women's affair, and for the rich and white.[28] The Pentecostal fostering of democratic participation was attractive to the faithful: each congregation chose its own pastor, and not so much for formal training as for strength of faith, religious eloquence, and a socio-economic situation similar to members'. In this community of sociability, every member was responsible for his or her own salvation as well as for the sustenance of the others, and women helped make decisions and recruit new members. Congregants built their own church physically and metaphorically, as in Barranquitas, where they were the "only church organization in town which [was] entirely supported by contributions of the local membership."[29] For the first time in Puerto Rico, people gained a sense of owning their religious institutions.[30]

As in other Protestant denominations, one was expected to behave according to the community's norms and eschew bad habits such as drinking, gambling, or adultery – the price to pay for the feeling of belonging and solidarity.[31]

The story of Don Taso, a cane worker born in the 1900s in the barrio Jauca of Santa Isabel, on the south coast, gives a striking example of wives' role in recruiting husbands, as much to control behaviour as to firm up faith. In the account he gave to anthropologist Sidney W. Mintz in the late 1940s and in 1952, Taso's conversion to Pentecostalism was the culminating point.[32] His narrative, and his wife's, offer a detailed description of conversions.

In 1950, Taso's eldest daughter attended an evangelization campaign held in Ponce by Brother Osborne, an American Pentecostal preacher, and told her parents of the cures he wrought. Taso's wife, Elizabeth, was next to attend, with her husband's permission. On her return Elizabeth also recounted cures and urged Taso to attend, knowing about his recurrent groin pain with incapacitating flare-ups. Taso finally decided to go to a Ponce meeting, where he felt an ecstasy and was cured but did not join on the spot, probably wanting to see whether his cure would last. His wife then made her own confession of faith, after trying the idea out on Taso. He later accompanied her to a local service and made his own profession of faith, enjoying the preaching and the hymns. Together they attended a night vigil in a neighbouring community where Elizabeth received the blessing. Taso received his own some days later, speaking in tongues and being infused with joy. The blessing is the first step in joining the church; on probation one learns the scriptures and "what one must do and what one must not do." In time the joy and thrill of the blessing decreased somewhat; Taso likened it to the passing of the intensity of falling in love.[33]

The Pentecostal dos and don'ts transformed the couple's daily lives and interactions. As Mintz summarizes it, Taso's conversion "required the deliberate surrender of certain prerogatives that seem to be tied to valued behaviour for males in his group: swearing, drinking alcoholic beverages, dancing, gambling, fornication, acquiring compadres, consensual union, delegating religious activity (if any) to one's wife, giving vent to violence in word or deed when the subculture's values for the individual are threatened, and non-deferral of gratification." It also required his wife to change behaviour, especially her fits of jealousy.[34] Conversion improved both their lives, as Taso acknowledged, and made them adhere to the values of "self-advancement in Western society": the deferral of gratification and the accumulation of capital for purposes other than gratification.[35]

SOCIAL FUNCTIONS OF PENTECOSTAL COMMUNITIES

Agosto Cintrón argues that Pentecostal communities in the island's interior replaced the informal communities of the *haciendas*, or large farms with tenant labour, that had given way after 1900 to large-scale sugar plantations.[36] This explanation for Pentecostalism's growth can be extended to the Depression era. Peasant or working-class Puerto Ricans could become Pentecostal ministers. The easy-going Pentecostal organization and religious practices made it attractive to the "poor and the marginalized." In Santa Isabel, in the 1940s, for instance, the cleavage between the Catholic and Protestant churches and the Pentecostal congregation was "quite noticeable ... The Pentecostal church concentrates on the poorer people."[37]

The Pentecostal churches, proliferating in the 1930s and 1940s, also attracted Protestants expelled from other denominations because of their charismatic expressions of faith or put off by the rigidity of their Protestant pastor, as happened in Comerío in the early 1930s.[38] But even mainstream Protestantism grew, and, if Comerío is typical, its members were more active and present in their church than Catholics; it also saw proportionately more men participate than the Catholic church.[39]

Some residents of Comerío left the Catholic church because the local priest charged fees for baptisms and weddings. One witness was distraught because his baby was sick and in danger of dying without being baptized. Others claimed that priests had refused to baptize illegitimate children, although the priests claimed to have baptized 125 illegitimate children in 1934. Be that as it may, there was now religious competition in Comerío as all over the island.[40] Initially in Comerío, people left the Catholic church for the Methodist because it was the earliest Protestant denomination in the community. But the Methodists saw some desertion from their ranks to the Pentecostal and the spiritists, showing, as one sociologist noted, "a tendency to individualize religious beliefs" and to "shop around" for a religious community.[41]

In Barranquitas, west of Comerío, Protestantism took many forms. The Baptists, granted the area at conquest, had a church building and "an imposing high school." Two Mennonite communities were recruiting and renowned for their "good works," especially "dental, medical, and eye clinics where they treat many people free and charge nominal fees to others." A small congregation of Pentecostals held nightly meetings "where they sing, play music, etc." But they were outnumbered by the *Espiritistas*, who met twice weekly.[42]

The advent of Protestantism in Puerto Rico after 1898 was a deliberate, systematic enterprise. It gave islanders a new experience of religion as community-building and mutual assistance. Evangelical denominations created communities that were close to the people and drew their legitimacy from the community rather than some hierarchy. It did not frown on an instrumental conception of religion. It accorded well with Puerto Rican popular cultural norms.

While Protestantism in its many forms took root, the Catholic church faced difficulties both with its manpower and with the social distance between clergy and faithful. This would make for long and arduous competition with Protestantism.

8

~

The Catholic Church and the State, 1930–70

AN AMERICANIZED CATHOLIC CHURCH

At the time of the conquest, only 21 per cent of Catholic priests were island-born. By one estimate, that figure had declined to 9 per cent in 1960.[1] Catholic clergy was increasingly made up of "young American priests who speak Spanish."[2] This was similar to the situation in Latin America.[3]

· A celebrated study of Puerto Rico in the late 1940s, directed by anthropologist Julian H. Steward of Columbia University, noted that the Catholic church was sustained financially by "donations received from the North American Church, from individual donors outside the small local parishes," and from returns on investments in real estate. Poorer communities had limited financial resources, and if the parish priest had income of his own from outside the church, this appeared to limit his sacramental influence over his parishioners. The church's reliance on outside revenue and on the financial support of local elites put it at risk of remaining an upper-class institution with little interest in "average" Puerto Ricans. In Santa Isabel east of Ponce, for instance, labourers saw Catholicism as the religion of "the upper class of hacienda owners and large merchants."[4]

The "average" Puerto Rican had little interest in the church as well, if Comerío can illustrate again. In the 1930s, more than half of the Comerío parish revenue came from outside the island. According to a local priest, "no one in town gives tithes and the largest donations are from seven to eight dollars annually. We receive about 400 dollars from baptisms. Collections from ordinary Sunday services are from three to four dollars. It is customary for the poor, as well as for many of those having more money, to put a silver or nickel coin in the collection box and take out change, when they do not have a smaller amount." The costs of annual religious festivals were borne by collections from brotherhoods and other religious societies. The local church spent $800 over the year for its activities. The local Methodist congregation, by contrast, spent $2,000 a year in religious work; two-thirds of the funds also came from the United States.[5]

The number of priests available to minister to the island's mainly Catholic population was small. In 1933, for instance, the diocese of San Juan had 126 priests (including the bishop) for 900,000 Catholics, or one priest for every 7,143 members. In Ponce, seventy-three priests (also including the bishop) ministered to 650,000 parishioners, or one for every 8,904 Catholics.[6] In the 1960s, it was estimated that the island had one priest for every 6,000 or 7,000 people, with only about 20 per cent being native Puerto Ricans.[7] By 1980, the ratio of priests to population declined to 1:8,000,[8] not that much better than the Dominican Republic's 1960 ratio of 1:11,000, one of Latin America's worst.[9] By comparison, the ratio of priests to Catholics in Quebec in 1962 was 1:586, or 11 times more than in Puerto Rico.[10]

The Catholic church considered education the foundation of moral conduct. It had not been able to counter the public-school system's refusal to teach Catholic beliefs to its charges, but anyway in 1931 only about half of the island's children attended school.[11] Private Catholic schools became popular among better-off families, who deemed them of better quality; they also taught English, believed necessary for advancement. By the 1970s, parochial schools were "bursting at the seams" as the demand exceeded the supply.[12]

RELIGION AND THE PUERTO RICAN IDENTITY

For anthropologist Sidney Mintz, Catholic ideology in Puerto Rico was "less expressed as an aspect of religiosity than as an aspect of national character." Beliefs and behaviour were defined with reference to Catholicism. Marriage or common-law unions, receiving or not receiving the sacraments, the belief in the supernatural powers of objects of veneration (holy images, statues, sites of "miracles"), the veneration of Mary as a saintly mother, and the division of women into saints or temptress "Eves," the public character of penance, the double sexual standard, all these were, for Mintz, signs of the cultural, rather than religious, character of Catholicism in Puerto Rico.[13] Even the evening recitation of the rosary has been viewed as a bond of national unity.[14]

Jorge Duany argues that these practices were common to Latin American popular religion,[15] but that does not mean that Catholicism was not part of the Puerto Rican identity, as it was, for example, until the 1960s of identity in Quebec, where Catholicism was the dominant religion, and where Catholic clergy controlled education, health and welfare, and exercised close control over the behaviour of its flock.[16]

CATHOLIC RELIGIOUS PRACTICE

Charles C. Rogler's sociological study of Comerío in the early 1930s provides some insight into popular Catholic religious practice. Out of about 14,000 baptized Catholics, the local parish priest estimated that 2,000 were "devout," attending services regularly. But Sunday Mass attracted about 400 people, or 3 per cent of the formally Catholic population. The priest also estimated that "the poor are more devout in their religious conduct than are the wealthier classes." Women made up 80 per cent of Sunday Mass attendance. Men, particularly of the upper class, considered religion to be *"cosa de mujer,"* a woman's thing. Inside the church, "the women of the upper class customarily sit in a group on the front benches on the left-hand side ... If the seats are full and a woman of the upper class enters, she will be given a seat by a member of the lower class."[17]

About 19 per cent of couples were in common-law unions, a rate lower than in the surrounding countryside. Consensual unions were "poor men's marriages": church services and weddings were too expensive for many. The lack of a formal church wedding did not affect couples' fidelity or their devotion to their children, which the sociologist observed was the same as for married couples. Birth and death rates were high, as was poverty.[18]

Sexual morality was very traditional. Women, whether single or married, were expected to be chaste: brides were to be virgins, and wives were to be faithful to their husbands, especially among the upper ranks of society. Men, however, could enjoy "sex freedom" within or outside their social class. These values were strongly internalized by men, but also by women, only half of whom thought men should be bound by the sexual norms imposed on women. This applied as well to the use of birth control: poor women, who bore on average seven children, had little knowledge of or access to birth control and believed that pregnancies were the will of God.[19]

Almost everyone in Comerío believed in the afterlife. "Even those who have committed major sins believe they will ultimately be forgiven and will find their everlasting resting place in heaven." There they would meet their departed friends and relatives, to whom the upper class bade farewell at death with solemnity, while the lower classes made more of a joyous occasion of it. with "eating and drinking and general merriment." Catholics also venerated the saints, particularly the parish's patron saint; this veneration was "the most holy, most aesthetic, most dramatic, and most ostentatious of all Catholic religious patterns in the community." Upper-class women believed the saints to be "intermediaries between us and God. They must be respected."[20]

Not so keen on veneration of the saints was the Catholic hierarchy, particularly priests of American origin, who saw the veneration of saints' statues as superstition.[21] But the practice continued well into the 1960s, at least among rural families, who held their own religious ceremonies such as recitation of the rosary and wakes where "the rosary is recited for nine consecutive evenings after a death." So did the practice of *promesa*: entering into a "contract" with a saint for curing sickness or to "bring a good harvest, or ensure business success"; in exchange, the supplicant would recite the rosary, wear special clothing, or attend Mass for a specified number of times. Failure to fulfil such a contract was said to entail eventual punishment, and, if the contract was not honoured before one's death, one's soul might be "compelled to wander until the obligation is redeemed."[22]

Another sociological study, conducted between July 1947 and January 1948, asked respondents about the place of religion in their life. The majority indicated that religion was important, but not the most important thing. Another third reported being religious "in their own way," while less than 1 per cent opposed or strongly opposed religion. More than 80 per cent of respondents identified as Roman Catholic, and a further 3 per cent as Roman Catholic and spiritist.[23]

These forms of religious identity did not translate into strong communal religious practice. The majority indicated that they attended religious services "occasionally," i.e., less than once a month. A quarter of males and 15 per cent of females declared never attending. This behaviour was more pronounced in larger cities and with older respondents. Nearly a quarter of men and women in an active union were in a consensual union or concubinage, and a majority of respondents agreed that couples in difficult economic situations had the right to limit the size of their family; for a further 13 per cent, all couples had the right to limit the size of their family.[24]

The celebrated sociological survey from the later 1940s, *The People of Puerto Rico*, included a detailed ethnographic examination of four pseudonymous communities selected for their diverse economic situations and later identified as Barranquitas and Ciales in the interior, Barceloneta on the north coast, and Santa Isabel in the south.[25] Although the study's four community monographs emphasized different aspects of religion – entitling the relevant sections "Religion" (twice), "Religion and Magic," and "Religion and the Supernatural" with a distinct section for "Magical Practices" – their observations were similar.[26]

The people of Barranquitas considered themselves "*muy católicos*," but their everyday life exhibited selective observance. About half of married people had civil or common-law unions. Birth control was frequent. Religious practice was a social occasion for the women, while men sought "their amusements in less formal ways and on more numerous occasions." Men's church attendance was low. The parish priest, who, unlike Protestant pastors, did not do much ministering outside the church, decried immoral behaviour, birth control, superstition, belief in ghosts, and spiritism. Veneration of the saints and the Holy Virgin was widespread. In rural areas, where priests seldom visited, residents took religion into their own hands to celebrate wakes and births in private homes. A small number of Protestants and devotees of spiritism lived in the urban parts of the community.[27]

The situation observed in Ciales was similar. Most of the population was nominally Catholic, "if not in practice." Protestants numbered fewer than two hundred. The church was an "organization to which they may have recourse at special and extraordinary times," and the priest "maintains but little contact with his flock." The church's three Sunday Masses attracted different clienteles by geography and class: the first Mass was for "the rural and the devout," while the two later services attracted upper-class members, especially women. In rural parts of the parish, veneration of the saints was the "dominant form of religious expression." Wakes, public recitations of the rosary, and promesas were common. The instrumental character of religion was also visible in the prevalence of spiritism, to which people turned "only when their personal security is threatened."[28]

The situation was also much the same in Barceloneta. The parish priest there – from the United States – remarked that his parishioners saw themselves as Catholic "because they were baptized" but admitted their ignorance of church doctrine and their lack of church attendance. Yet there too, the cult of the saints and the custom of promesas were evident to the anthropologist. She also noted the interest in magical practices, devoting several pages to it, and included spiritism under that heading. The Barceloneta study also noted a few Evangelicals and Pentecostals.[29]

In Santa Isabel, working-class people were "nominally Catholic." Baptized and to be buried as such, they occasionally went to Mass, had pictures of the saints in their homes, but "rarely marry by Catholic ceremony" and seldom went to confession or received communion. They made fun of the parish priest for his dress and "Spanish accent" and viewed Catholicism as "the church of the rich." A small minority, mainly middle class in the urban part of the community, adhered to established Protestant churches or to Pentecostalism.[30]

Some of the religious customs described in the four community monographs are noted by later observers. For example, "in Puerto Rico as in Latin American countries, religious baptism of the children is a social event having little to do with the religious background of their parents in many of the cases." Marriages, while "important social events," were "a discriminatory index of profession of faith,"[31] signalling adherence to Catholic precepts. Rural families continued to venerate *santos* and crosses in their homes and carried on the tradition of wakes, public recitations of the rosary, and promesas.[32] Promesas often pertained to the wearing of *hábitos*, special white clothing that marked the wearer publicly. One scholar noted that this practice extended to non-practising Catholics and was part of popular religion in Puerto Rico.[33] Spiritism, too, continued to draw adherents, more as a supplement to Catholicism than as an alternative.[34]

Another student of folk culture in the later 1940s conducted interviews with nearly 1,700 participants in over sixty communities. His 1952 publication recorded the popular practice of Catholicism, Catholic popular expressions of belief such as the veneration of saints, the feasts of the cross, the sung rosaries, and Christmas celebrations and songs. The author transcribed sixty-six folk prayers to obtain all kinds of favours from various saints or members of the Holy Family, as well as popular spiritist practices.[35] A similar study, conducted in 1958, noted that among the favours sought were prosperity, winning the lottery, or gaining the interest of a man,[36] all examples of a very instrumental conception of religious practice that had Spanish antecedents.[37]

Among the popular expressions of faith reported in the 1952 study were the stories of the apparition of the Virgin of Monserrate in Hormigueros, a popular story involving a late-sixteenth-century landowner (a basket weaver in the oral tradition compiled in the 1940s) of Catalan origin encountering a wild bull and praying to the Virgin for the bull to be stopped in its tracks; the Virgin appeared and the bull was duly stopped.[38] The Hormigueros shrine was built by the landowner in gratitude to the Virgin and led to the creation of the town.[39] In recounting her youth in Moca, near Aguadilla, in the early 1950s, Ana Maria Díaz Stevens gives a vivid account of family and communal religious practices of people seldom able to attend services, which required a "three to four hour expedition," sometimes after obtaining a ride to public transportation on an oxcart. She labelled this form of Catholic practice "Oxcart Catholicism."[40]

Marian devotion reached a fever pitch in Puerto Rico in 1953. On 25 May, the expectation of an apparition by the Virgin Mary in Barrio Rincón of Sabana Grande, east of San Germán, drew 100,000–150,000 pilgrims – roughly one-sixth of the island's adults – from "all parts of Puerto Rico and from such other far off places as Haiti, the Dominican Republic, Cuba, Miami and New York." The Virgin was said to have appeared to primary-grade children in Barrio Rincón as they had gone to fetch some water at a well near their school, and to have announced that she would appear again on 25 May. No apparition was forthcoming, but many visitors claimed to have witnessed miracle cures.[41]

The idea of Marian apparitions was very much in the air. The movie *The Miracle of Our Lady of Fatima* (Warner Brothers, 1952) was playing on the island, though not in Sabana Grande, and attracted a lot of viewers.[42] During May, radio and television frenetically covered the apparitions and the expectation of more, as well as stories of cures by faith. It was also a time for sociological assessment: "The pilgrims represented every one of the major categories of the population – though the proportionate representation could not be ascertained," and "the vast majority of the crowd believed, to one degree or another, in the events as reported." Many hoped to be cured with "water from the well blessed by the Virgin."[43]

Through sermons and in print, the Catholic hierarchy expressed doubts about the apparitions and the "miracles."[44] The church's dim view of popular religious practices needed better spokespeople, as the practices obviously retained their appeal. During our 2011 visit to the site of the Virgen del Pozo apparition, a letter by Cardinal Ratzinger (later Benedict XVI) in his quality as Prefect of the Congregation for the Defence of the Faith relieved the faithful of their obligations towards any promesa they made to obtain a favour from the Virgin or from a saint.

Government, too, sought to channel popular behaviour. In the spring of 1953, it posted signs throughout Barrio Rincón warning that, as the water from the well near the children's school did not come from "water plants controlled by the Health Department," it should be boiled before being drunk, to which one pilgrim remarked sarcastically that "what they should do is put water from the well in the aqueduct."[45] Today, the well is enclosed by a small fence, so that one cannot drink from it. Instead, a pipe carrying government water is offered as a substitute, which some visitors use as such (see figure 8.1).

The sorts of popular religious practice observed in 1940s fieldwork and around the apparitions of 1953 attracted attention in the 1960s. The residents of Loíza, east of San Juan, considered themselves either "folk" Catholics,

Figure 8.1 A pilgrim taking water from the government pipe below the
Virgen del Pozo, Sabana Grande, March 2011.

"who emphasize baptism, *promesas*, the saint cult, novenas, and the ceremonial cycle," or formal adherents who attend Sunday Mass and "conform
to church teachings." Women were much more numerous at Sunday Mass
than men and made the Daughters of Mary the largest religious association
in the parish. Still one in five marital unions was common-law. Loíza was
also the home of 523 Pentecostals, who formed nine congregations and represented 80 per cent of local Protestants.[46]

Catholicism remained dominant in the 1960s. A 1962 island-wide sample
put the proportion of Catholics at 77.1 per cent, Protestants at 17.5 per cent,
and 3.8 per cent "without religion." A survey of a Bayamón neighbourhood
in the same period had an almost identical breakdown.[47]

By the 1970s Sunday church attendance seemed higher among Catholics.
"In some places it may be as high as 30 per cent," noted one observer; "as

people move from the interior into more populated areas, it takes time and patience to make them realize their duty to assist at Holy Mass every Sunday." The same commentator also saw "a great upsurge" in consecrated marriages. Public processions for recitation of the rosary, veneration of the saints, promesas, and the wearing of *hábitos*, which "at times ... are mixed up with superstitious beliefs and hopes," remained common practice.[48]

NATIONALISM AND POLITICAL ACTION

Perhaps some of the resurgence in the orthodox practice of Catholicism had to do with its being defined as an integral component of *puertorriqueñidad*, the expression of Puerto Rican national identity propounded by Luis Muñoz Marín and the Popular Democratic Party he founded in 1938 and that propelled him to be the island's first elected governor in 1948. Muñoz Marín, wrote literary critic Luis O. Zayas Micheli, "injected a moral and religious direction to his Popular Democratic Party." He defined Puerto Ricans as religious and Catholic, whence emerged their sense of nation, with both inextricably intertwined. From a more radical perspective, Pedro Albizu Campos, the brilliant Ponce mulatto who obtained a law degree from Harvard University in 1922, returned to his hometown to practise labour law, and became leader of the Puerto Rican Nationalist Party in 1930, defined Catholicism as an integral part of the national identity that had to be defended against American imperialism through independence, a struggle that turned violent between the 1930s and the 1950s.[49] As this sentiment developed, it paradoxically highlighted the Catholic hierarchy's "foreign" origins.[50]

The Catholic church became more distant from Puerto Ricans as it came to oppose the highly popular Muñoz Marín. Their confrontation began before he even entered politics. In 1922, when twenty-four years old, using a pseudonym, he proposed birth control as a means of combating poverty in his father's newspaper, *La Democracia*, and in 1923 he did the same under his own name in a different publication. Bishop Jorge José Caruana answered that birth control was "race suicide" and a mortal sin and that the topic ought not to be discussed in public. Birth control was also illegal under US and Puerto Rican law.[51] During the New Deal beginning in 1933 under President Franklin Roosevelt, Puerto Rico began to offer birth-control information, over the protests of the US and Puerto Rican Catholic hierarchy. Five years later, the legislature authorized the Health Department to offer birth control throughout its health clinics, as well as eugenic measures to sterilize feeble-minded or sick women.[52] These programs were popular. In the 1940s, 7 per cent of women were sterilized, and in the 1950s, public hospitals carried out 6,317 sterilizations and distributed 300,000 contraceptive devices.[53]

The Puerto Rican constitution, overwhelmingly approved in a referendum in March 1952 under the aegis of Muñoz Marín, enshrined the right to "non-sectarian public education" and provided for the "complete separation of church and state," prohibiting use of public funds for private schools. The US Congress then amended it, notably to exempt students in private schools from compulsory public-school attendance, and the amendments were approved during a referendum held with the election of November 1952.[54] During the election campaign, the bishop of Ponce, James Edward McManus, issued a leaflet stating that Muñoz Marín's Popular Democratic Party (PPD) had been "the enemy of Catholic ideals for many years" and that to vote for it was a mortal sin that would entail excommunication. The bishop commented privately on the fact that the governor had lived in "concubinage" for many years and thus lacked the moral authority for his office. Despite its bishop's condemnation, Ponce voted nearly 60 per cent for the PPD.[55] Some PPD supporters dressed up in cassocks to celebrate their victory and mockingly recited the rosary for the souls of the losers.[56]

The church again condemned the PPD in the next election. In 1960, besides calling a vote for the PPD a sin, since the party "permitted legally the practice of birth control, divorce, and eugenic sterilization, as well as encouraging common-law marriages,"[57] it launched the *Partido Acción Cristiana*, composed mainly of upper-middle-class professionals, business people, and intellectuals. The party drew only 6.6 per cent of the votes.[58] As the PPD argued in each election, a vote against the church was not a vote against the Catholic faith, but against clerics who stepped out of their religious duties.[59]

THE CHURCH CONFRONTS
LIBERATION THEOLOGY

In the 1960s, liberation theology, a Latin American movement that sought to return to the core of Jesus' message, the defence of the poor against oppression, arrived in Puerto Rico's Catholic church.[60] In Comerío, Dominicans trained in Holland, a locus of theological innovation, and who ministered to the local parish, rejuvenated liturgical practices. They said Mass in the vernacular and borrowed from Latin America the practice of singing the liturgy to local folk music. The local version,[61] composed by one of the Dominican fathers, William Loperena, a noted Puerto Rican musicologist, was called the *Misa Jíbara*.[62] Moreover, the Dominicans shared pastoral work with the local Methodist minister. They also used US federal funds to produce local arts and crafts and thus help preserve folk culture and put together programs for industrial and agricultural workers.

The Comerío clergy was also known to favour independence for Puerto Rico, and Loperena, for one, did not hide his support for the Puerto Rican Socialist Party, which favoured armed revolution to overthrow US rule. When Rafael Grovas Felix, the bishop of the new diocese of Caguas (1965) visited Comerío to seek donations for his new see, the parish refused to contribute because of extreme poverty. He was also told that Christ would not have wanted the bishop to live in a palace apart from his humble flock.[63]

In a sermon for Three Kings' Day 1970, Loperena argued that, as Jesus allowed the Three Kings to come to him without prior declarations of faith, so should the congregation welcome, in a similar manner, Cuban revolutionary leader Che Guevara, should he now enter the church to pray. That was the last straw for many conservative Catholics, who viewed the comparison between the Three Kings and Che Guevara as heresy. In the summer of 1971, the bishop ordered the Dominicans to leave Comerío. The Comerío faithful sided with their clergy and simply closed the church. They even demanded explanations from the bishop, in vain. When the bishop of Ponce suspended the Dominicans from their Yauco parish for the same reasons, parishioners there also closed their church.[64]

Ironically, Grovas Felix was responsible for Antulio Parrilla Bonilla's being consecrated bishop. Parrilla Bonilla would become the most persistent proponent of liberation theology among Catholics in Puerto Rico, as

well as an opponent of American colonialism, an advocate of independence, a socialist, an activist against the Vietnam War and the military draft,
a protester against the US navy's use of the island of Vieques for military
training, and an active proponent of the cooperative movement.

Born in San Lorenzo in 1919 into a large lower-middle-class family (his
father was a mason and store owner), Parrilla Bonilla did his secondary
schooling in Caguas and worked in the sugar-cane industry as a weigh-
scale operator. In 1939, he moved to New York, where he did odd jobs, then
returned to undertake a degree in commerce at the University of Puerto
Rico. He was drafted by the US army in 1943 before he could complete his
studies and was deployed in Panama as a radar technician. By then he was
already an advocate of socialism and of Puerto Rican independence. Some
of his army comrades in Panama were devout Catholics, and he "converted"
to Catholicism after reading about St Theresa de Jesus. Upon his return to
Puerto Rico he decided to enter the priesthood. He received his seminary
training in Maryland from 1946 to 1952, and later joined the Jesuit order
and did his Jesuit novitiate in Havana, Cuba, from 1957 to 1959. He had been
encouraged by Pedro Albizu Campos to join a regular order to "escape the
jurisdiction of the North American prelates in Puerto Rico."[65] He took his
vows in September 1959 and was assigned to a Puerto Rican parish in lower
eastern Manhattan. In 1960, he was transferred to the parish of St Ignatius
of Loyola in Río Piedras. The following year, disappointed by his superior's
lack of pastoral experience, he asked his bishop for another assignment and
was put in charge of the archdiocese's Office of Catholic Social Action,
which he led until 1965, when Bishop Grovas, as a condition for accepting
the new see of Caguas, requested that Parrilla Bonilla be named his auxiliary
bishop. Parrilla Bonilla was consecrated bishop in August 1965.[66]

In July 1966, however, Grovas requested that his colleague leave his diocese. According to the archbishop of San Juan, Luis Aponte Martínez, both
men were strong-willed *independentistas*, but with divergent views about
pastoral work.[67]

Parrilla Bonilla retained his title of bishop, and in 1966 the Puerto Rican
conference of bishops offered him the rectorship of the Ponce joint diocesan seminary, troubled by bad administration and poor candidates. In 1967,
he merged the Ponce seminary with the Jesuit seminary of Aibonito and
left the direction of the new institution to the Jesuits. He sought missionary

work in Guatemala but was not accepted by its archbishop. The leader of the Puerto Rican Independence Party, Gilberto Concepción de Gracia, convinced him in 1968 that he should help the island's people in their fight for freedom and justice rather than do missionary work in some other country. The archbishop of San Juan suggested to him that he return as head of the Apostolate of Social Work, but Parrilla Bonilla requested to be made auxiliary bishop of San Juan, presumably to have some latitude in his work; the archbishop refused. In his account of this episode, Parrilla Bonilla made clear that he did not expect the archbishop would have supported his social and political positions. Instead, in 1968 Parrilla Bonilla found a teaching position at the Institute of Cooperation at the University of Puerto Rico in Río Piedras, while he assisted with pastoral work in local parishes. He also helped in ministry work at the Hormigueros basilica.[68]

It became clear, in 1971, that Parrilla Bonilla could expect little support from the island's conference of bishops, which stopped inviting him to its reunions. Without a formal church appointment and material support, he joined and became head of the John XXIII Social Center, in Río Piedras, which disseminated the late pope's ideals on social justice and human rights and worked for rejuvenation of the church along the lines set out by him and the Vatican II Council. Parrilla Bonilla worked tirelessly to this end: he wrote newspaper articles, gave conferences in Puerto Rico and abroad, built a library, created a *comunidad de base* – a local group of clergy and faithful doing religious education, pastoral and social work among the poor, somewhat like the work of Protestant Evangelical communities – fostered cooperative movements, denounced capitalism, colonialism, and imperialism, participated in the International Conference of Solidarity with Puerto Rican independence, helped migrants, offered support to conscientious objectors, all the while providing pastoral services at the Center and elsewhere. He did not shy from linking the Catholic hierarchy in Puerto Rico to the US oppressor and its threat to the survival of the Puerto Rican nation.[69]

Perhaps the most famous of his public stands occurred in 1979, when he took part, with other religious figures and with independentist leaders, in ecumenical prayers for local fishermen on a Vieques beach. This was a way of confronting the presence on the island of the navy, which had declared the beach off-limits because of its live-munitions exercises. Twenty-three demonstrators were arrested. The confrontation made front-page news, which highlighted the presence of a bishop and of a reverend among those arrested. Parrilla Bonilla was the first to appear before a federal judge, who gave him a one-year suspended sentence and a $500 fine, which he refused to pay. A newspaper article suggested that the bishop perhaps thought himself above the law because of his clerical title, to which he replied that transgressing an unjust law was not an ecclesiastical privilege but the moral duty of any man of conscience.[70]

Puerto Rico boasted other strong-willed liberation theologians in the 1960s and 1970s. In *Los católicos rebeldes en Puerto Rico durante la guerra fría*, José Enrique Laboy Gómez catalogues the actions of the Jesuit Salvador Freixedo, the author of *Mi Iglesia duerme* (My Church Is Asleep), a virulent 1969 denunciation of the church's inaction against the island's severe social and economic problems. Laboy Gómez also recounts the stances of other Jesuits and Dominicans, Trinitarian priests, nuns of the Good Shepherd and of the Sacred Heart, Carmelite nuns, and missionaries of the Holy Trinity.[71]

Liberation theology led two female orders to work with the poor rather than educate the daughters of the local bourgeoisie. In 1970, the Sisters of the Sacred Heart, inspired by personal training in Latin American liberation theology, decided to close their prosperous Santurce boarding school in order to concentrate on aiding the poor. The Carmelites' Vedruna school, in Guaynabo, suffered the same fate in 1977, for the same reasons.[72]

The Catholic hierarchy responded with vigour to liberation theology. Laboy Gómez's last chapter, "Persecutions against radical Catholic groups in Puerto Rico," runs to eighty pages.[73] Father Loperena was demoted from his post; the bishop of Ponce prohibited the singing of Loperena's *Misa Jíbara* and instead reinforced traditional Spanish hymn music.[74] The bishop closed the Ponce seminary, where seminarians had post-Vatican II hopes of more collegial decision-making. The Catholic hierarchy stuck to its pre-Vatican II ways and practices.[75] Suspended from his pastoral duties, the Jesuit Freixedo eventually left the priesthood. In 1976, the archbishop of San Juan, Luis Aponte Martínez, rebuked the Carmelites for closing their Guaynabo school and arranged for the local parish to take it over. The hierarchy had the support of influential conservative Catholics, the local police, the Federal Bureau of Investigation, and, in some cases, it seems, of the Central Intelligence Agency.[76]

In 1960s Puerto Rico, liberation theology was not exclusive to the Catholic church. The Evangelical Seminary in Río Piedras, just across from the University of Puerto Rico, was also host to this movement,[77] which was soon denounced as leftist political subversion led by Baptist minister Samuel Silva Gotay.[78] Silva Gotay was working for "rejuvenation" of Evangelical practice through active political stances in favour of decolonization and against the excesses of capitalism. He was accused of being a tool of Cuba's Fidel Castro-style communism and was forced out of the ministry.[79] Silva Gotay went on to an examination of Latin American liberation theology (published 1981), and in 2014 he received an honorary doctorate from the Evangelical Seminary.[80]

In the mid-twentieth century, even with help from US Catholics, the church in Puerto Rico responded poorly to the spread of Protestantism, particularly Evangelical. It failed to change the communal religious practices of "nominal" Catholics. Its sparse and mostly US-origin secular clergy did not help breach its social and physical distance with the laity. The church aligned with the most conservative parts of society and its forceful putdown of progressive elements confirmed this alignment. In the following years, the Catholic church would also face two other monotheist religions, the Jewish and Muslin faiths, as well as forms of Christian worship over which it had little control.

9

Varieties of Monotheism: Protestants, Jews, and Muslims in the Late 20th Century

The Catholic church of Puerto Rico in the late twentieth and early twenty-first centuries continued to face challenges to its religious hegemony. A 2017 compilation of "all religious groups in Puerto Rico" by the Latin American Socio-Religious Studies Program (PROLADES by its Spanish acronym) identified 126 such groups, from the Eastern Orthodox to the "marginal Christian," Buddhist, Hindu, Animist, and "psychic-New Age." Though an undercount (only one Jewish and two Muslim communities), it suggests the diversity of religious affiliations today.[1] The most socially visible affiliations, by date of earliest appearance, were Evangelical Protestantism, Judaism, and Islam. Their new communities of the soul would increasingly challenge the concept of Catholicism as a foundation of Puerto Rican identity.

EVANGELICAL PROTESTANTISM

Since the 1960s, Protestantism, especially in its evangelical form, has grown in Puerto Rico as elsewhere in Latin America.[2] In the mid-1960s, Protestant communities on the island were said to number over 500 and to have close to 250,000 members, or about 10 per cent of the island's residents.[3] By 1985, this proportion had risen to 27 per cent, the highest in the Spanish-speaking Caribbean and Latin America.[4] In 2008, Protestants were estimated to make up 30 per cent of the island's people,[5] and in 2014, 33 per cent, according to the Pew Research Center, second only to Catholicism, at 56 per cent.[6]

Protestantism's attraction in Latin America has been linked to socio-economic changes that have increased social fluidity and redefined personal and social identity. Pentecostalism is "quick and easy" to adopt. It requires no long initiation or training, is simple to understand, allows individuals to immediately believe in themselves, and retains the "magical" aspect of religion that characterized popular Catholic practices. Its ministers are locals, its practitioners are usually poor or middle-class persons who have experienced social or geographical dislocation, and it focuses on concrete problems such as lack of work, family tensions, alcoholism, or drug consumption.[7] Across Latin America, Pentecostalism was the dominant form of Protestantism.[8] In Puerto Rico, half of the 1,700 respondents to the 2014 Pew survey who answered the question about being Protestant defined themselves as Pentecostal. Overall, one-fifth of all respondents described themselves as Pentecostal, with eighty-two of them stating they belonged to a Protestant church other than Pentecostal.[9]

Pentecostalism brings together old and new. A renowned sociologist of religion remarks that "it unites the ancient layers of solidarity with the kinds of expansive organizational principles recommended by specialists in church growth. And the Pentecostal preference for stories, for gesture and oratory, belongs simultaneously to pre-literate and to post-literate society." He also notes the similarities between Caribbean cultural practices and those of Pentecostalism: orality, informality, spontaneity, and flexibility, traits observed in Haitian Pentecostalism, for example.[10]

In Puerto Rico, Pentecostal congregations have also been viewed as recreating old social links and relationships, which had disappeared with the *haciendas*, where the *jíbaros* had lived and worked.[11] A sentiment of communal solidarity was surely comforting, but may not indicate a desire to return to earlier forms of social organization. Pentecostal congregations were largely free of the hierarchy and exploitation characteristic of *haciendas* and strove to provide communal help not only for the soul but also for the body.

Pentecostalism has been linked to Americanization, as it "serves to maintain a socio-cultural system which though dynamic is becoming less Puerto Rican and more American" by its advocacy of "'good' work habits, puritanical standards, and relatively conservative social and political views." By aiming to improve members' social and economic situation, it also seeks to compensate for the failure of "modern" society to do so.[12] In Loíza, for example, "techno-economic changes have been primarily responsible for the emergence of a class system – i.e., groupings of individuals who share the same life chances – which is quickly replacing the traditional status groupings."[13]

Protestantism in general may also serve as a way station to middle-class propriety: some adherents, on joining the middle class, return to the Catholic church favoured by the affluent elite. Religious affiliation could sometimes be an instrument of social ascension.[14]

Women's place in religious communities, Protestant as well as Catholic, was central. They made up the majority of respondents to the Pew survey who affiliated with a religion; two-thirds of Protestants were women.[15] More women than men (81 per cent against 70) declared religion very important in their lives.[16] Two-thirds of women, against only one-third of men, whether Catholic or Protestant, reported giving a percentage of their income to the church.[17] The same difference was observed for frequency of prayer: three-quarters of women prayed at least once a day, compared to only three in five men. Inversely, of the sixty respondents who said they never prayed, two-thirds were men.[18]

Conversion is a substantial phenomenon among Puerto Rican Christians. The Pew survey reported that 22 per cent of Puerto Ricans were no longer members of their childhood religion; 38 per cent of Protestants had been raised as Catholics. Among the reasons cited for conversion were a greater personal connection with God (70 per cent of converts), style of worship (63 per cent), and more help for members (41 per cent). More than half of Protestants, versus 17 per cent of Catholics, gave a percentage of their income to the church.[19]

Women are central in the conversion from nominal Catholicism to active Protestantism, as they usually convert first (as with Taso's wife, in chapter 7) and become very active in liturgy.[20] The use of native clergy and of local popular music gives evangelical Protestantism a Puerto Rican identity.[21] "Through their informal visits and contacts, Puerto Rican Protestant ministers have achieved the kind of close relationship with the people envied but never known by the Catholic priests."[22]

Loíza may again illustrate the Pentecostal sense of community. Members "frequently see each other during the course of the day, whether it be to visit the home of a sick 'brother,' to proselytize, to conduct a prayer vigil, or to perform some other social or religious function."[23] Acceptance required an "extended probationary period during which the newcomer has something specific to aim for: a personal experience of the Spirit."[24] This hardly impeded membership, as in 1979 there were an estimated 225,000 island Pentecostals.[25]

To join the community, one had to declare one's faith, which included Christian beliefs and specific Pentecostal articles, such as baptism "subsequent to a clean heart" through immersion, and the speaking of tongues. Candidates could attend religious services practically every day of the week: women conducted the service on Monday, the Youth League did Tuesday, and the Men's Society Wednesday, while Thursdays and Fridays were for visiting homes of "delinquent members or 'interested' individuals who either specifically ask for a service or who politely acquiesce to a communicant's request." Services began with a devotional component of "prayers, hymns, Bible readings, solos, testimonials, 'sermonettes,' collection of voluntary contributions, and discussion of church business." The "*mensaje*," or sermon, was not reserved to the local pastor; it could be given by a "guest preacher, or some designated member of the congregation." Services at the homes of recently deceased members resembled traditional folk Catholic wakes, but without alcohol. Syncretism, however, had its limits: spiritism was "vehemently denounced" as the handiwork of the devil.[26]

Membership required an official marriage. To take Loíza as an example again, member couples were all wedded "either at a Pentecostal or civil ceremony." Extramarital sex was forbidden and, when recurrent, provoked expulsion. As well, divorce was allowed only on grounds of adultery. Behavioural prescriptions were not always followed regularly, as some men converted to please a prospective wife, only to return to the cafés, the "street," and extramarital activities after marriage. Women were held to their traditional role of "inconspicuous, modest, and faithful" wives.[27]

Other forms of revivalist folk religious practice were manifest. One was the Prophets movement, a "uniquely Puerto Rican folk religion." A Caguas group, the Cilicia Temple, attracted anthropological study in the early 1960s.

The group drew on North American fundamentalist Protestantism, Puerto Rican spiritism, Catholicism, and lower-class Puerto Rican folk culture. Its particularity lay in the ceremonial wearing of veils by its female members, prophesying, and faith healing by "anointing with olive oil, exhortative prayer, laying on of the hands, and massaging." Besides bodily healing, this procedure was said to protect from evil spirits. Ceremonies were marked by informality and "spontaneous and total audience participation coupled with a high degree of emotionalism," with singing or music playing.[28]

Cilicia Temple members numbered in the forties, and the men belonged to the "urban proletariat" of non-farm wage earners, most of them earning between $100 and $200 a month. The group required a very strict way of life: no "smoking or using tobacco; drinking alcoholic beverages, fornication out of wedlock, attending or participating in athletic events; gambling or attending cockfights; strolling in the town recreation plaza for social purposes; dancing or attending parties; and such feminine practices as the use of artificial beauty aids (i.e., cosmetics, padded brassieres, stylized hairdos, etc.) and wearing provocative clothing." Structurally, it constituted a "spiritual community of equals" where everyone had a role in religious ceremonies.[29]

As the anthropological study noted, "Cilicia can be conceived of as a socio-religious sub-system within the framework of the larger social system – with its own set of values, norms, status and roles, and behaviour patterns competing with and to some extent replacing those of the larger social system in the lives of individual members."[30] The remark may apply to most Evangelical congregations in Puerto Rico: sociologically, their appeal is a sense at once of distinctiveness from the wider society and of community within the congregation. They answer needs that the Catholic church is weakly set up to address. We see in the next chapter other forms of religious practice that developed to attract popular attention.

JEWISH COMMUNITIES

Jewish communities emerged in the twentieth century in Puerto Rico, said to be the only Caribbean island with congregations representing the three main strands of Judaism. Adherents now number an estimated 1,500.[31] The Spanish crown, which had expelled Jews from Spain in 1492, forbade non-

Catholic immigration to its colonies until 1870, and even after that date the local Catholic church frowned on it. Nevertheless, some "converted" Jews are known to have lived on the island from 1519 onwards.[32] Some settled in the mountainous areas, practised their former religion in secret, and had to profess to be Roman Catholics in public.[33] Others were traders: in the first half of the nineteenth century; for example, Ponce had Jews from Curaçao.[34] Some traders came from the nearby island of St Thomas, such as Isaac Louis Jacob Bravo, who had to "convert" to Catholicism in order to marry a Catholic. He was a respected member of the Mayagüez community and a friend of Puerto Rican nationalists Ramón Emeterio Betances and José de Diego.[35] Other Jews were living in Guayanilla, on the south shore, in Aguadilla, and in Mayagüez.[36] A few took part in the 1868 Grito de Lares insurrection and were executed by the Spanish authorities.[37] The 1898 census noted the presence of American Jews in Ponce.[38]

The first sizable presence occurred in the wake of the US conquest, as Jewish-American servicemen remained on the island. They formed "the core of a nascent Jewish community in the southern town of Ponce. Colonel Noah Shepard served as an unofficial leader of this group, and Rabbi Adolph Spiegel, who had served in the US forces, remained in Ponce for several years. Many of these Jewish former servicemen worked in Puerto Rico's administration, helping to create its legal code and court system, and worked in public health to help eradicate tropical diseases from the island."[39] Almost immediately the Jewish newcomers became involved in improving the island's legal, social, and health conditions.

US immigration restrictions in the 1920s impelled many eastern European Jews to consider Cuba and Puerto Rico as way stations into the mainland, and some eventually settled on the islands. In Puerto Rico, Jewish entrepreneurs operated tobacco manufacturing companies, made furniture, sold food and supplies, and ran diamond and leather-good factories, "mostly in Caguas and Cayey." A number worked as doctors, members of medical faculties, and public-health advocates. The first Jewish community centre and synagogue date from this period.[40] By 1940, there were "only 150 known Jews in Puerto Rico." Jewish refugees from Nazism opened a community centre in 1942 in the Hato Rey district of San Juan. In 1954, the Conservative Shaare Zedek (Gates of Justice) synagogue was established in San Juan's Miramar neighbourhood.[41]

After 1945, Puerto Rico industrialized on a large scale, as the island's Operation Bootstrap provided incentives for investment in local industries. American Jews took a notable part in the process, launching factories making mahogany furniture, leather goods, bedding, underwear, and cigars and setting up the first supermarket chain, Pueblo. The 1960s saw Jewish investment in tourism, particularly in large seaside hotels.[42]

Fidel Castro's 1959 Communist revolution in Cuba prompted another wave of Jewish immigration. A number of Cuban Jews transplanted their businesses, in commerce, residential construction, and banking. Many of these immigrants were Orthodox or Conservative. From this time on, the island's Jewish community (mainly in and around San Juan) increasingly took on a Spanish flavour. During the next decades, more Spanish-speaking Jews arrived from Argentina and, to a lesser extent, Colombia.[43]

Like most other religious groups in Puerto Rico, the three synagogues sustain communities of the body and of the soul. The oldest, the Conservative Shaare Zedeck, has its synagogue and community centre in Miramar. It is housed in a large private residence acquired in 1953 and remodelled twice since. Besides the synagogue, the compound – the Jewish Community Center of Puerto Rico, created in 1942 – includes a Hebrew school, a library, a kosher store, administrative offices, meeting rooms, a children's play area, and a ballroom.[44] The Conservative synagogue has about two dozen persons for Friday services and about forty on Saturdays. Services are held in English or Spanish; the community is now mainly Spanish-speaking. In recent years, members of this congregation have suffered from the island's economic difficulties, and their numbers were declining even before Hurricane Maria and the government's financial difficulties.[45]

The Reform community, Beth Shalom (House of Peace), was constituted in 1967 and established a centre a year later, across the street from Shaare Zedeck. In 1972, it purchased a building in Santurce, which it converted into a synagogue. It has boasted a series of distinguished rabbis, mainly from the United States.[46] It provides "spiritual and educational activities" to a "diverse, multigenerational, multicultural, inclusive community with an emphasis on social justice, education and dynamic experiences in Judaism." It is financed by a "combination of dues, donations, school fees and fundraising programming,"[47] but, like the Conservative congregation, it struggles financially with the exodus of some members to the mainland, for which recent converts, now the bulk of the community, have not completely compensated. Between twenty and thirty persons attend the Friday services and about sixty on Saturdays, and Hebrew, Spanish, and English are used.[48]

The third Jewish congregation is Orthodox Chabad-Lubavitch. It runs the Rohr Jewish Center in the Isla Verde district of Carolina, east of San Juan, close to the airport, major tourist hotels, and beaches. Chabad of Puerto Rico was founded in 1999 by Rabbi Mendel Zarchi, originally from Brooklyn, NY, and his wife, Rachel.[49] Zarchi is now the longest-serving rabbi on the island. In the first years, Chabad-Lubavitch conducted services in rented facilities. It began construction in 2013 of its new quarters,[50] inaugurated in August 2016. It provides education in Hebrew and the Torah, sells kosher food, and offers community services. The congregation is composed of about seventy families of Puerto Rican, American, or Israeli background. It also welcomes thousands of visitors from the United States and the Caribbean each year.[51]

Shabbat services there draw from thirty to sixty people. When I attended a service in early 2019, I counted about thirty men (a traditional partition separated the women from the men), and more than sixty men, women, and children attended the Kiddush lunch afterwards. The service was conducted in Hebrew, with some English. The community appears well established, and Rabbi Zarchi is optimistic for the future of both his community and Puerto Rico in general.[52]

The Holocaust monument installed in 2012 in front of the Capitol building, on Avenida de la Constitución, is a symbol at once of the cooperation among the three Jewish communities of San Juan, who commissioned and paid for it, and of the open attitude and generosity of the officials who supplied the site. It is, according to Rabbi Norman Patz, who has studied Holocaust monuments across the world, one of the most remarkable. Its curved sheet of steel represents a torn fragment of a Torah scroll, which on its left side twists into a chimney recalling the smokestack of a crematory oven. The flame-shaped Hebrew letters at the top mean "remember," while the cut-out silhouette of a family at the bottom personifies the victims of the Holocaust and the descendants they did not have. The inscription reads, in Spanish and English, "Let six million candles glow against the darkness of these unfinished lives" (see figure 9.1).

Figure 9.1 The Holocaust monument in front of Puerto Rico's Capitol,
on Avenida de la Constitución, San Juan, 2019.

To the right of the monument, one finds the "Path of the Righteous," a
serpentine alley with plaques commemorating non-Jews, including Oskar
Schindler, who helped save Jews during the Second World War. To the left,
a series of plaques in a curved space honours Puerto Ricans killed in the
terrorist attack on Israel's Lod (now Ben Gurion) airport in 1972. The site
thus remembers Jews and non-Jews, from Puerto Rico and elsewhere, sym-
bolizing the bonds between them.[53]

ISLAMIC COMMUNITIES

It is said that the first Muslims reached the island with European explorers, but too few to form communities. Muslim Spaniards – merchants,
slaves, explorers – arrived in the Caribbean.[54] West African slaves brought
to Puerto Rico to work in sugar-cane plantations in the sixteenth and

seventeenth centuries hailed from Muslim regions of Africa, despite the crown's repeated attempts to keep them out. But the prohibition of non-Catholic religions prevented Muslims from passing on their faith to their island descendants.[55]

It was not until after 1945 that a number of Muslims settled in Puerto Rico. The Muslims of Río Piedras grew from Palestinian families who arrived from various parts of Latin America, where they had moved following Jewish settlers' 1948 displacement of Palestinians. Others came from Jordan, Egypt, Lebanon, Turkey, or Africa. Many were merchants or traders in clothes, textiles, and jewellery, or ran pharmacies and restaurants. By 2013, Muslim Puerto Ricans included doctors, engineers, and university professors.[56]

Estimates vary of the number of Muslims today. In 2008, *El Nuevo Día* reported about 5,000 members, mostly immigrants from Palestine, Egypt, Lebanon, and Syria.[57] One scholar also estimated 5,000 for 2010.[58] The American Community Survey of 2012 suggested 2,528, which the imam of the Montehiedra mosque rounded up to 3,000.[59] The same cleric put the 2015 figure at 3,500, 500 of them Puerto Rican converts.[60] These variations in estimates are quite understandable, given Muslims' geographical mobility on the island and with the mainland.

A 2010 survey detailed eight mosques or Islamic centres. The oldest was set up formally in Río Piedras in 1981 in a converted three-storey dwelling. A second was established in Ponce in 1987, with two hundred places for men and twenty for women. A 2012 observer noted that the Friday service there attracted only one-fifth of capacity.[61] A large mosque was opened in Vega Alta, on a hill not far from the main highway, in 1992: it has room for 1,200 men and 120 women. A small one was set up in Jayuya, in the mountainous centre of the island, the following year. Fajardo and Hatillo mosques were established in 1995 and 1998, respectively, Fajardo's with fifty places for men and fifteen for women, and Hatillo's with room for two hundred men and thirty women. A small centre was set up in Aguadilla in 2002, and a centre on a large piece of land in the Montehiedra suburb of San Juan in 2007, for four hundred men and fifty women.[62] A different source mentions that in 2011 Loíza had a small mosque, for twenty people.[63] In 2015, the imam at the Montehiedra mosque mentioned two mosques in the San Juan area, Río Piedras and Montehiedra, as well as eight elsewhere on the island, in Aibonito, Fajardo, Hatillo, Jayuya, Moca, Ponce, Vega Alta, and Yauco. Moca and Aibonito were not on the 2010 survey, while Aguadilla and Loíza no longer appeared to have a mosque.[64] Again, population mobility may explain the varying numbers of mosques during the period, but it is striking how Muslims established a presence across the island.

During a Friday prayer ceremony in Río Piedras in 2015, I counted more than sixty men, from youngsters to elderly men. (Women were in a separate room.) Prayers and sermons were conducted in Arabic; the imam was a scholar from Alexandria, Egypt, who did not appear to speak either Spanish or English. In early 2019, the young imam of Montehiedra estimated about seventy attendees at Friday prayers, and Vega Alta's imam about twenty.[65]

Puerto Rico's Islamic centres are Sunni,[66] but there are also Shias, mystical Sufis, and a proselytizing Ahmadi community.[67] Weekend schools in some of the Islamic centres teach Arabic and Islam to young Muslims.

As happened to the Jewish community and Puerto Rico in general, for Muslims the deteriorating economic situation has somewhat reduced numbers,[68] which loss converts are not likely to make up for. The Muslim communities are at once closed and bound by the Arabic language, and open and well integrated into local neighbourhoods. Most members look like other islanders; they speak Spanish as natives and interact daily with their neighbours. Their relative invisibility ensures that they are not feared or branded as radical Islamists, as those I spoke to attested, and as did the two imams I interviewed in early 2019.[69]

But this is perhaps an overly rosy picture painted for the sake of appearances. Some Puerto Rican converts to Islam (or "reverts," as some call themselves, in the belief that they are returning to their ancestors' faith) have a hard time finding acceptance both among Arab Muslim settlers and among the general population. Some Arab Muslims view the island as degenerate because of the drinking, singing, dancing, and general gregariousness; they are contemptuous of converts who retain some of these cultural practices, so some of the latter feel like second-class Muslims. Ordinary Puerto Ricans, unaware of local Islamic communities, are wont to consider Muslim converts as foreigners, not "real" Puerto Ricans. Converts tend to avoid mosques, teach themselves Islam, and home school their children. To develop their identity as Puerto Rican Muslims, they learn about the Muslim presence on the island, which antedates the arrival of sizable numbers of

Arab migrants since the 1950s.[70] This is their way of making Islam indigenous to Puerto Rico.

The story of antiques dealer Irso Reyes may illustrate the ambiguous relationship between Muslim converts and their relatives and neighbours.
Reyes began to investigate Islam as a religion in the wake of the terrorist
attacks of 11 September 2001 in the United States. He was attempting to give
meaning to his spiritual life. As a Muslim convert, Reyes was labelled a terrorist by his neighbours. But converting to Islam led him to abandon drinking, stop wearing fancy clothing, stop "thieving," and marry the woman he
was living with. His parents, who had been ashamed of his conversion, now
loved him "madly." The story of Reyes's post-conversion behavioural transformation parallels that of Taso (see chapter 7).

Another convert, an anthropologist and computer engineer, also reported her family's shame at her conversion. Her husband told of his leading classes on the Qur'an in his garage, stressing that the mistreatment of
women was an Arabic cultural tradition rather than a Muslim one. These
converts, interviewed by *El Nuevo Día*, insisted that what mattered was to
follow the five pillars of Sunni Islam – faith, prayer, charity, fasting, and the
pilgrimage to Mecca – and be *"buenos musulmanes puertorriqueños"* (good
Muslim Puerto Ricans).[71]

In the second half of the twentieth century, religion in Puerto Rico became
even more diversified, but the three forms of monotheism examined in this
chapter were simultaneously acquiring specifically Puerto Rican "colour,"
as more and more of their members came from the dominant island culture. The need to insert these new religious forms into Puerto Rican culture
was also manifest, and what it means to be "Puerto Rican" was broadening
to encompass religious diversity. This efflorescence of religious practices
seems not to have caused the kind of social friction it has elsewhere in the
world. Indeed, non-institutional forms of religious practice have also flow-
ered, as we see in the next chapter.

10

~

Non-Institutional Forms of Religious
Practice in the Late 20th Century

Since the 1960s, two trends have continued to shape religious practice in
Puerto Rico. The first is the Catholic church's ambiguous, or conflicted,
role within society. For some authors, the church was the site of "the con-
tradictions, the dichotomy, the crises which the unequal relationship between two societies [Puerto Rico and the United States] produces in the
dominated one."[1] The church was thus a sort of microcosm of Puerto Rican
society. For other writers, the church's siding with the political status quo,
making it "*antiindependentista*" and "*antipuertorriqueña*," ensured its decline even as the independence movement itself was losing steam. The rise
of messianic movements drawing the faithful away from the church was a
sign of profound and widespread social changes.[2]

The second trend, examined in this chapter, is the persistence of popular
forms of religious practices not apart from, but alongside formal religious
structures. This trend is hard to reconcile with the anomie interpretation
of religious behaviour that grounds analysis of the first trend. Popular devotions and ritualistic practices survived even as society became better ed-

ucated and better off. An international survey indicated the highest level of religious belief in all of Latin America.[3] According to Jorge Duany's 1998 assessment, popular Catholicism, in its veneration of iconographic objects, in everyday speech, and in oral tradition, maintained a strong influence on the Puerto Rican mind. It articulated basic Christian values such as equality, reciprocity, and justice, even though it might deviate from orthodox doctrine. As with other religious traditions, it was concerned with the immediate problems of the dispossessed in society, namely poverty and illness.[4] Traditional religious belief was grounded in popular devotions and practices sustained by great interest in religious shrines and the attractive force of apparitions, but also by radio and television. This mingling of old and new in popular religious practice is characteristic of the island.

Some Puerto Ricans also engaged in rituals derived from African religion such as *santería* and *brujería* (withcraft) and found the appropriate artefacts in *botánicas*, drugstore-like shops that sold such products and dispensed advice. Spiritism, which had arrived in the nineteenth century, continued. This all attests to the growing diversity of religious practices.

POPULAR CHRISTIANITY

In the 1970s, about fifty Cheos brothers continued to foster popular piety in the mountainsides. Some were married, some were single, some even took the vow of celibacy. They were *campesinos* (peasants) "trained to give the basic and necessary instructions for the receiving of the sacraments."[5] They also visited homes, led people in reciting the rosary, and generally were "at the service of any priest who may want them to work, for any length of time desired." They were firmly under the guidance of the clergy and received "an intensive training course."[6] They perpetuated a tradition of lay involvement in the church among residents of the island's interior. As well, one of the children who had seen the Virgin at Sabana Grande in 1953 began "his messianic mission" in the 1980s and, by 1990, had recruited more than 400,000 devout followers of the Virgin.[7]

In mid-1986, a survey on devotion to Mary was mailed to various places in Puerto Rico. Out of 500 questionnaires sent, 172 responses were received. Respondents were asked the preferred name they used for the Virgin Mary.

"Our Lady of Perpetual Succour" was the most popular. Not all respondents were Catholics, but of the eighty-five who answered the question on weekly attendance at church, four out of five declared weekly or daily.[8]

Celebrations of the Holy Cross (*fiesta de Cruz*), or novenas, held for the nine days, usually in May, between Ascension and Pentecost, remained popular well into the late twentieth century. Novenas took place mostly in private houses in cities, with a home altar bearing a crucifix and an image of the Virgin, the events accompanied by popular music and sung rosaries.[9] In San Juan, novenas attracted many people, but the Catholic clergy stayed away, except perhaps to offer a Mass before they began. People of all ages took part in the singing wakes of the novenas, a festive social occasion as much as a religious observance.

In Manatí, west of San Juan, one man organized the fiesta de Cruz in his own home, obtaining the city's permission to close off part of the street for the nine days. The whole neighbourhood assisted in decorating the altar and in preparing refreshments, sandwiches, and sweets. The gatherings were a major event, drawing older people, who were seated, and youngsters, who tended the kiosks where everything was free. One observer noticed strong religious devotion, even though the local priest considered the fiesta a "pagan celebration."[10]

In Loíza, where many residents are descended from slaves, the feast of Santiago (St James the Apostle, of Compostela), on 25 July, also affirmed popular will in religious matters, as the official patron saint is St Patrick. The Santiago feast runs over ten days, with three days of processions in honour of each of the town's three statues of St James. St James was invoked in Spain in the fight against the Moors, and in the New World Spanish settlers enlisted his help to repel attacks by the natives or by English invaders. St James also helps repel other forms of attack, such as physical illness. The occasion has a carnival-like atmosphere, with four masked and costumed characters: the Caballero, who stands for St James; the Vejigante, a grotesque stand-in for the evil Moors; an old man; and the *loca* (crazy woman), impersonated by men dressed in drag; younger participants evoke characters from "popular science fiction, war, and horror movies."[11] As a response to the attraction of local Baptist and Pentecostal congregations, the Catholic church created the parish of Santiago Apóstol in 1971.[12]

In Aguadilla, each July, local fishermen organize a procession in honour of the Virgen del Carmen over the waters of the bay to be blessed with good luck and be protected at sea. It is considered bad luck to swear while at sea.[13]

The practice of making *promesas* to the Virgin or to the saints continues. It is considered a sacred undertaking, and failure to carry it out can condemn a person to purgatory. If a person becomes ill or dies before executing the promesa, the family must do so. In the same vein, the *Velorio de Reyes*, or the wake before Three Kings' Day, remains a notable form of devotion in rural areas; it consists of a sung rosary as thanks for favours obtained from God, the Virgin Mary, or the Three Kings.[14]

Religious shrines continued to draw visitors and gain in status. The church of Our Virgin of Monserrate, in Hormigueros, was recognized by the pope in 1998 as a minor basilica, acknowledging a miracle there and its many visitors (see chapter 8). The church is situated on top of a hill with narrow streets, full of shops, bars, and restaurants that cater to visitors, and, within the church, statues of the Holy Virgin and her child are both dark-skinned, as elsewhere in Latin America (see figure 10.1). In Puerto Rico, the "Black Madonna" of Monserrate "is the most common theme of all the *santos* or native carved wooden images of all times"[15] and symbolizes integration of "native people of colour into Catholic society."[16]

Apparitions, as well, still made local news. *El Mundo* of 17 May 1978 reported on an apparition of the Virgin Mary in Lares. On 18–20 April 1986, the island's press reported an apparition of the Virgin in Naranjito, in the island's interior.[17]

As centuries-old popular religious beliefs and practices persisted, modern technology provided new means of diffusion. In 1917, the Redemptorist fathers had launched a monthly publication, *El Mensajero del Perpetuo Socorro*, which linked groups of Marian devotees. After 1945, this devotion took to the airwaves.[18] From the 1930s on, the Catholic church used radio to transmit religious programs. It was joined, on radio station WNEL, by the Evangelicals, who bought airtime and were required to submit their sermons for vetting a week ahead, to ensure no prejudice to the Catholic church. By 1940, one of every seven households in Puerto Rico owned at least one radio, placing most islanders in contact with "city values." By 1948, eighteen Protestant radio programs were aired weekly, with producers pay-

Figure 10.1 Statue of the Vírgen de Monserrate, Hormigueros basilica,
10 February 2008.

ing the broadcasters. The first entirely religious radio station opened in
Vieques in December 1956, broadcasting in English and Spanish. The first
Spanish-only religious station began in 1974 with financial support from
the island's Evangelical communities; three more opened in 1982. The

Catholic response came the following year, with mainly music on the FM band, talk radio on the AM band, short religious "commercials," and religious programs only on Saturdays and Sundays. A survey of listeners showed that religious radio filled an emotional need for some people and served rather to comfort and strengthen their beliefs and attitudes than to change them.[19]

In October 2018, a guide to licensed radio stations in Puerto Rico listed twenty-four Spanish-language religious stations among the 133 outlets.[20] A similar listing labelled thirteen of the island's thirty-six TV stations as religious.[21] Religious broadcasting also turned to podcasting, creating the most podcasts from 2013 to the end of 2017.[22]

POPULAR FAITH HEALING

"Unorthodox" religious practices and beliefs also persisted as the twentieth century wound down. Santería became more visible with the arrival in the 1960s of Cuban exiles.[23] Field research in the 1970s showed that santería "priests" were men and women of average education and social class, who remained Catholics.[24] This fusing of Catholicism and African-inspired beliefs, practised among Taíno centuries earlier, might confuse theologians, but it resembles additional term insurance on top of regular life insurance, answering specific needs not covered by the latter. Most practitioners looked for it to give meaning to their life, to answer the call of the saints, or to solve health problems, the last being the most cited reason for joining.[25] Among the divinities of santería were Shangó, god of manhood, storms, and the sun; Yemeya, goddess of the seas; Obatala, master of purity and intelligence; Eleguá, master of man's destiny; and Oshún, god of arts and passions. (In Cuba, these deities were also given names of the Virgin or of the saints.) *Santeros* believed in reincarnation and in communicating with the dead. Initiation into the rites was expensive, estimated at $1,500.[26]

Botánicas are shops that sell "books, candles, and the many paraphernalia relating to Santería and Espiritismo."[27] They exist all over the island, particularly in the north (see figure 10.2). In August 2018, a Yellow Pages–like web site dedicated to small and medium businesses listed sixty-one,[28] and another thirty-seven.[29] Eighteen appeared on both sites, for a net total of eighty. Many bear the names of saints, while others' hint at African origins

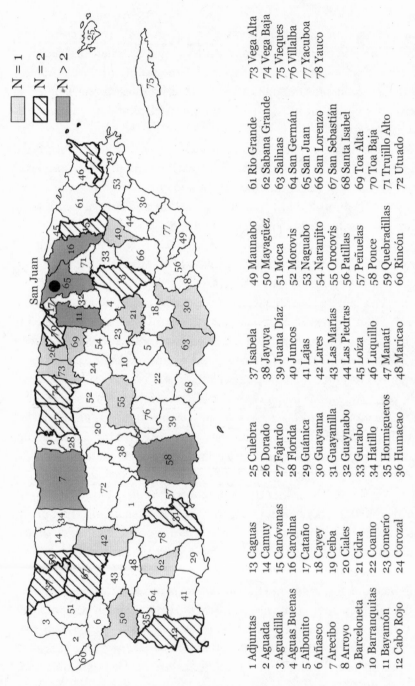

Figure 10.2 Number of *botánicas* advertising in Yellow Pages–like web sites, by municipality, 9 August 2018.

N = 1
N = 2
N > 2

San Juan

1 Adjuntas
2 Aguada
3 Aguadilla
4 Aguas Buenas
5 Aibonito
6 Añasco
7 Arecibo
8 Arroyo
9 Barceloneta
10 Barranquitas
11 Bayamón
12 Cabo Rojo

13 Caguas
14 Camuy
15 Canóvanas
16 Carolina
17 Cataño
18 Cayey
19 Ceiba
20 Ciales
21 Cidra
22 Coamo
23 Comerío
24 Corozal

25 Culebra
26 Dorado
27 Fajardo
28 Florida
29 Guánica
30 Guayama
31 Guayanilla
32 Guaynabo
33 Gurabo
34 Hatillo
35 Hormigueros
36 Humacao

37 Isabela
38 Jayuya
39 Juana Díaz
40 Juncos
41 Lajas
42 Lares
43 Las Marías
44 Las Piedras
45 Loíza
46 Luquillo
47 Manatí
48 Maricao

49 Maunabo
50 Mayagüez
51 Moca
52 Morovis
53 Naguabo
54 Naranjito
55 Orocovis
56 Patillas
57 Peñuelas
58 Ponce
59 Quebradillas
60 Rincón

61 Río Grande
62 Sabana Grande
63 Salinas
64 San Germán
65 San Juan
66 San Lorenzo
67 San Sebastián
68 Santa Isabel
69 Toa Alta
70 Toa Baja
71 Trujillo Alto
72 Utuado

73 Vega Alta
74 Vega Baja
75 Vieques
76 Villalba
77 Yacuboa
78 Yauco

(Yoruba) or mysterious powers (La Milagrosa, El Gran Poder, Simple Solution, La Fuente, La Gitana). Some have their own web site, while others manage Facebook pages or produce YouTube videos, as a Google search on www.google.com.pr for "botánica puerto rico" will reveal. Even as they support traditional healing practices, botánicas have adopted contemporary channels of communication.

Belief in witches continued well into the twentieth century, particularly in the island's interior. Over five hundred interviews conducted from 1968 to 1974 and again in 1987 gathered numerous, richly detailed stories from informants across the island, but especially from old people living in the interior. Most respondents appeared to believe in witches, but even those who did not could recall the stories told by their parents and what they used to do to protect themselves. Witches were usually depicted as old women, ugly, obnoxious, dishevelled, and thin. They flew at night on their broomsticks, especially on Tuesdays and Fridays, to go and play tricks on people, changing shape into animals or children, stealing small sums of money, gathering together to provoke heavy rainfalls that would damage crops, or tricking sailors into running their boats aground. The stories collected included descriptions of witches' practices to cause illness or death, to cause other forms of mischief, and formulas to make someone fall in love; they also explained how to recognize and catch witches, methods to defend oneself from their evil spells, and ways to cancel spells.[30]

Another way to defend oneself from physical illness or psychological problems is to see a *curandero*, or traditional folk healer, who will take a holistic approach to help effect a cure: herbs, massage, counselling, and prayer. *Curanderismo* is a widespread Latino traditional healing system that is still practised in Puerto Rico, though perhaps in danger of extinction.[31]

Spiritism, too, retained its attraction, keeping up the belief in the spirit world and adapting its flexible beliefs and practices to the current day.[32] It shared the homegrown, eclectic, and syncretic character of botánicas, santería, and brujería, and was often conflated with these practices. One scholar noted, with apparent disdain for its practitioners, that "its eclectic sponge-like quality is perhaps its greatest asset in the struggle to survive among so many competing religions; it seems to attach to its system, and popularize for its adherents, whatever social and philosophical new ideas have greatest

current appeal to some of the more troubled segments of Puerto Rican society."[33] Another observer has described *espiritismo* as a "community healing system" and an "important mental health resource for Puerto Ricans."[34]

The *People of Puerto Rico* collective study of four communities in the late
1940s noted that "the great majority of spiritualists remain formally within
the body of the Catholic church. Spiritism is especially characteristic of
those middle and upper-class people who seem unwilling to lose their social
status as Catholics by associating themselves publicly with beliefs often
characterized as lower class or ascribed to country people."[35] The sociologists who visited Barceloneta in the 1940s noted magic everywhere and that
"many [rural] persons claim to be both Catholics and spiritualists, or
Protestants and spiritualists."[36] In Ciales, spiritism was prevalent among
"the agricultural workers and small farmers, who live in the context of dis-
solving traditional ties, as in Sabana; the town lower class; and elements of
the new middle class whose background and motivation are similar to those
which Protestantism reaches."[37]

In the early 1950s, spiritist leaflets could be purchased for between
twenty-five and fifty cents in convenience stores, newsstands, public mar-
kets, and libraries, where they accounted for a large proportion of sales.[38]
In the late 1950s, over a third of respondents in a follow-up study of
Barceloneta saw spiritism as pervasive within the older generation and perceived a "resurgence among all social classes," although the author proffers
no evidence for the "resurgence" other than his observations during the
1940s and in 1959–61.[39] The work offers a useful description of spiritist
mediums' healing "*séances*" and explains spiritism's popularity as "a sign
of collective insecurity provoked by confused and unreliable situations in
the structure of communal existence" brought about by US colonization.[40]

Socio-economic factors also helped explain the prevalence of spiritism
among Puerto Rican communities in the United States. Studies of such
communities in New York noted that from 30 to 80 per cent of interviewees
had recourse to a medium for various emotional and physical problems.[41]
Poverty, lack of education, and social discrimination deterred access to
orthodox health care, as an anthropological study of a Puerto Rican neighbourhood in the Bronx documented; approximately half of the seventy-
nine households and half the adults in the sample were adherents of
spiritism.[42] Spiritist *centros*, where mediums performed healing rituals,

facilitated social interaction and mutual assistance. "For many members, the centro becomes the focus of social activity in their lives."[43] Respondents used spiritist healing as a form of short-term therapy "during crisis or transitional periods." Problems included difficult relationships within the family or on the job, "the death of a close relative; life transitions (puberty, menopause, and terminal illness); vague anxiety manifested in mania, nightmares, and the like; and physical complaints for which the person has not received satisfactory medical attention." Spiritism also provided a form of social identity that facilitated social links with newcomers,[44] much as belonging to the Knights of Columbus did in upper-class Catholic circles. The community's spiritism included both Kardacian and *santería* practices, which varied across centros, although most respondents saw little difference, as they "had at one time or another consulted mediums of both persuasions."[45]

An anthropological study of Loíza in 1964 noted that "spiritualism like Pentecostalism or, for that matter, conversion to any of the different Protestant churches, is one of a number of alternatives which a person may choose when confronted with a serious problem." A local spiritist, female as most spiritist mediums were, became known for her curative powers and conducted home "*séances*" and gave private consultations. She also warned her customers against *envidia*, envy felt by others that was linked to witchcraft, fear of which was "not uncommon" in the community.[46]

Belief in the transformative powers of religion, whether it be apparitions of the Virgin, the effectiveness of promesas, the speaking in tongues of Pentecostal converts, or the healing power of herbal potions and of spiritist "*séances*," continued to demonstrate, among late-twentieth-century Puerto Ricans, a utilitarian form of syncretism with little formal theology. Communities of the soul continued to provide succour even as they became more numerous and offered a broader range of possible affinity.

~

Conclusion

From time immemorial, religion has been a fundamental part of Puerto Rican society. The Taíno conceived of the physical world and of its inhabitants in religious terms. The gods had created the material world and the supernatural world, and the gods affected daily life. Interactions with the gods served to heal and protect. The social fabric was interwoven with religious significance. In Spain at the time of the conquest of Puerto Rico, and for centuries afterward, popular religion exhibited similar traits: it conceived of the world as having been created by God, who could be seen at work in nature and among humans. Spaniards asked Jesus, Mary, and all the saints to negotiate with God in their favour. In Spain, however, formal Catholicism imposed a hierarchical and authoritarian framework on religious practice that commingled with the state to delineate the bounds of proper thought and behaviour. Authority, both religious and secular, was conceived as emanating from God's will.

This was the basis on which Spain established its state religion in the New World. Various theological positions were used to justify the treatment of natives and of the slaves brought over from Africa. There was divergence about the means to convert these groups, but not on that objective. Spain constituted Puerto Rico and the Lesser Antilles as a bishopric under the direct control of the monarchy. Regular clergy was mobilized to serve the small settler communities on the shores of the island and to carry out missionary work in the interior. Among the settler communities, popular religion retained the characteristics it exhibited in Spain: an instrumental concept of the supernatural marked popular religious practices. As in Spain, formal Catholic rites were practised unevenly, and the scarcity of priests meant little social control over the *criollo* population.

The nineteenth century saw little increase in the church's power. The number of parishes rose as population grew around the island and progressively into its interior. The building of churches was a community effort financed in part by municipal and state subsidies. But this visible appropriation of public space – the churches anchored the *plazas* in the centre of town – did not expand the church's control over social space. In fact, the hierarchy, mostly loyal to the imperial government that supplied it with funds and personnel, grew doubtful about criollo allegiance to the monarchy and relied more and more on peninsular clergy. The *peninsulares* did not share their parishioners' criollo culture, and they sometimes exploited them in league with merchants and landowners from Spain. Furthermore, parish priests' behaviour sometimes deviated markedly from Catholic norms. Social distance between clergy and laity grew, compounded by the physical distance between settlements and parish churches, reducing lay frequenting of sacraments: attending Mass could be sporadic, and common-law unions frequent, because of steep wedding fees. Baptism, which signified the joining of the community of Christians, and the burial ceremony, which marked the passing to the community of departed souls, were the only inescapable sacraments. Yet there was ardour in popular manifestations of devotion such as erecting domestic altars to the saints, reciting the rosary in public, taking part in the activities of *cofradías*, and attending public celebrations for the Three Kings' holidays or for a patron saint. Private recitations of the rosary and the making of *promesas* to the Virgin Mary or to a saint in exchange for a favour remained as instrumental religious practices.

Spain's transition to parliamentary monarchy in the nineteenth century challenged the Catholic church in Puerto Rico. Financial support from the state fluctuated with the constitutional changes in Spain. Church properties on the island were confiscated to reimburse slave-owners for the abolition

of slavery. Earlier in the century a cash-starved government seized the religious orders' monasteries. The Puerto Rican church's control over all legal
marriages was lost as civil unions were allowed in the 1880s; its control over
burials was also challenged by the authorized presence of non-Catholics
on the island.

During the same period, the Catholic church confronted ideological
challenges from anti-clerical and liberal thought and from the arrival of
other forms of worship. Nationalists were inspired by liberal movements
in Europe and by the Latin American push for independence in the early
nineteenth century. They rejected Spanish domination over the colony and
church domination of its inhabitants. They took to the printing press to
publish books and articles, to the consternation of ecclesiastical authorities
who replied in kind. Protestant parishes were established in Ponce and in
Vieques, and Protestant missionaries began to proselytize. Freemasons and
spiritists also challenged the Catholic church's religious hegemony.

These challenges were compounded by the US conquest in 1898 and the
separation of church and state that the conquerors imposed. Catholicism
could no longer be taught in public schools, and the state would no longer
support the church financially. Most of the Spanish-born regular priests
returned to Spain. The church had to rely on US regular orders to replenish
its ranks, including the position of bishop. Of a different culture, and sometimes language, this new clergy could only increase the social distance with
the flock that had developed over the previous century.

American and Puerto Rican Protestants ran the island's new administration, but popular religious practice continued the customs of previous
centuries. The weakness of the Catholic church allowed the appearance of
spontaneous lay Catholic preachers, who aimed at keeping Puerto Ricans
away from non-Catholic religious practices and bringing them back to a
life closer to the precepts of the church.

The conquerors expected that Americanization would convert islanders
to Protestantism. US Protestant denominations saw Puerto Rico as new
territory to evangelize. They divided up the island and set up congregations, schools, hospitals, and welfare institutions across the island. These
early congregations belonged to the "historical" Protestant denominations,
but they were joined in 1916 by Pentecostals, who would later in the century become the largest Protestant church. Protestantism placed religious

practice firmly in the hands of the individual, who had to study the Bible and participate in his or her congregation's instructional, devotional, and social activities in order to be considered a member of the community. Some Protestant communities imposed tight social control over members, cutting them away from the larger culture and instilling in them a new social identity.

From the 1930s to the early 1970s, the Catholic church continued to contend with the problems it had faced earlier in the century. It relied on US Catholics for manpower and financial resources and received little of either. The ratio of priests to population remained low. Catholicism was perceived as the religion of the upper classes, particularly of women. The church's opposition to Luis Muñoz Marín, the charismatic founder of the Popular Democratic Party and governor 1949–65, cemented this impression in the population. Sociological studies of the 1940s and 1950s attested to the continued distance between the Catholic clergy and its flock, infrequent sacraments, as well as the persistence of popular religious practices and their strong communal nature. The church had little influence over these practices. In the 1960s, it by and large failed to keep up with the changing times, when being a Christian increasingly meant fighting for the poor and un-educated and challenging the institutions of oppression such as capitalism and imperialism. It repressed the manifestations of liberation theology among its clergy.

The Catholic church also failed to check the rise of other creeds. By 2014, a third of Puerto Ricans identified as Protestants, and more than half of those considered themselves Pentecostals. Jewish communities, present since the Second World War, built synagogues and community centres in the San Juan area. In the last decades of the twentieth century, Islamic communities took root along the northern part of the island, in numbers greater than the Jews. Rites of faith healing, whether of African or European origin, continued to attract those who needed help with their problems.

The Catholic church maintains a strong institutional presence across the island. At the beginning of the twenty-first century, reports an anthropologist, it conducted ministries in "hospitals, nursing homes, prisons, orphanages, shelters, and homes for unwed mothers." More formally, it sustained chapels in hospitals, prisons, nursing homes, the airport in Carolina, and even police stations.[1]

But the Catholic church is in difficulty. The archdiocese of San Juan has sought bankruptcy protection for failure to properly fund its Catholic school teachers' pensions.[2] More significantly, the proportion of Puerto Ricans who describe themselves as Catholic decreased from 70 to 56 per cent between 2010 and 2014. Younger islanders look for spiritual inspiration more in social causes than in traditional religious belief.[3] They are part of a trend among Latin Americans.[4] In 2019, there were calls to perpetuate the tradition to visit seven churches during Holy Week,[5] and the major San Juan newspaper, *El Nuevo Día*, saw fit to emphasize that the tradition remained strong despite secularization.[6] But it also reported, on Easter Monday, that police had arrested 428 persons during Holy Week for drunkenness and drug use,[7] underlining how religious celebrations were also occasions for social revelry.

I draw from this short history of religion in Puerto Rico two major themes that run through this rich and diverse experience. The first is an instrumental conception of religion. At the level of belief, the sacred serves as an explanation of the unknown: where does one's society come from, how to account for the forces of nature, how to understand the afflictions one encounters, where does one go after life on this planet? In everyday life, religion provides the framework and strategies for making bargains with the supernatural (from cemís to deities to saints) to overcome the problems of one's life. This was evident among Spanish Catholics when Spain first colonized Puerto Rico. On the island, religious beliefs and practices were refashioned in a syncretic way, taking symbols and customs from Taíno, Yoruba, Christian, and "scientific" (spiritist) sources and mixing them into individual or collective combinations that could fluctuate as need and circumstances changed.

The second theme that I draw from this historical survey is the shaping of religion by informal communities of the soul. In Puerto Rico, we can speak of religion of the people, by the people, for the people. From the outset, religious practice has been shaped more by local people than by formal hierarchies. Among the Taíno, for example, the *behiques* remained intermediaries with supernatural powers only as long as the community recognized that status. The hierarchical structure that the Spanish Catholic church instituted on the island held little power outside of the major cities, and in rural areas people developed their own forms of worship, deriving individual practices from collective forms of devotion. Protestantism, especially in its Pentecostal guise, rested on informal communities of adherents who chose their own pastor for his involvement in the community as well as his spiritual eloquence.

As someone from Quebec, where Christian religious practice has become essentially invisible in the public sphere, I am struck by the persistence of collective and individual religious practice in contemporary Puerto Rico. I notice it among my friends and relatives on the island, but also when visiting shrines, synagogues, and mosques, or churches on patron saints' feast days. Turning on the TV or the radio, one encounters a multitude of stations dedicated to religion.

In these early decades of the twenty-first century, then, religious life in Puerto Rico remains vibrant in increasingly diverse forms. The island's need for community does not abate, even with the existence of social media, as the response to Hurricane Maria has revealed, when local populations bent on self-help set up food-producing cooperatives and community improvement groups.[8] Religion, in its multiple embodiments, will continue to fulfil the need for spiritual community.

~

Notes

PREFACE

1   Bell and Sahgal, *Religion in Latin America*, 51, 56, 40, 43, 14.
2   My CV is available at https://igartua.uqam.ca.
3   Igartua, "Quebec and Puerto Rico," 34–61.
4   See as examples the varying definitions in the French, English, and Spanish definitions of religion in Wikipedia: https://fr.wikipedia.org/wiki/Religion; https://en.wikipedia.org/wiki/Religion; https://es.wikipedia.org/wiki/Religi%C3%B3n. On the 26 September 2018 access date, the first two announced no scholarly consensus on definition, a conclusion the third denied.
5   Anderson, *Imagined Communities*.
6   See for instance Picó, *Historia general de Puerto Rico*; Scarano, *Puerto Rico*.
7   Bell and Sahgal, *Religion in Latin America*, 14.
8   Juan F. Caraballo Resto interview.
9   Diaz Stevens, *Oxcart Catholicism*.
10 Rafael L. López Valdés, email, 21 February 2020. See López Valdés and Alegría, *Pardos y morenos esclavos y libres en Cuba*. Professor López Valdés has been teaching a course on Afro-Caribbean religions at San Juan's Centro

de estudios avanzados de Puerto Rico y el Caribe (https://ceaprc.edu/wp-content/uploads/2019/10/programacion-de-cursos-agosto-2018-primer-semestre-2018-2019.pdf, accessed 24 June 2020).

CHAPTER ONE

1 There is some scholarly argument about the proper use of the word "Taíno." William Keegan, in "The 'Classic' Taíno," 71, sees a cultural distinction between the "contact-period peoples of Hispaniola and the Turks and Caicos Islands," whom he labels "Taíno," and suggests lower-case "taíno" for all the Indigenous people of the Greater Antilles and Bahamas, because of the "enormous cultural diversity." But he concludes, "If we recognize that culture is chaotic, and its configuration is always changing, then 'Taino' is just a name that needs to be more specifically defined in each use." I use it here to refer to the Taíno of Puerto Rico. Elsewhere Keegan stresses the use of the singular to refer to the Taíno as a people, a usage he adopted as co-editor of *The Oxford Handbook of Caribbean Archaeology* and which I also adopt here.

2 Hobsbawm and Ranger, *The Invention of Tradition*.

3 Stevens Arroyo, "Indigenous Elements," 100; Schroeder et al., "Origins and Genetic Legacies."

4 Curet and Stringer, *Tibes Indigenous Ceremonial Center*.

5 Keegan, "'Classic' Taíno," 71; Oliver, *Caciques and Cemí Idols*, 216.

6 Keegan, "'Classic' Taíno," 79, citing Oliver, *Caciques and Cemí Idols*.

7 Stevens Arroyo, *Cave of the Jagua*, 252.

8 Oliver, *Caciques and Cemí Idols*, 53.

9 Stevens Arroyo, *Cave of the Jagua*, 252.

10 Ibid.

11 Pané and Arrom, *An Account*, 13–14.

12 Oliver, *Caciques and Cemí Idols*, 133.

13 Pané and Arrom, *An Account*, 6.

14 Ibid., 17.

15 Stevens Arroyo, *Cave of the Jagua*, 243.

16 Oliver, *Caciques and Cemí Idols*, 59.

17 Pané and Arrom, *An Account*, 25–6.

18 Ibid., 64.

19 Loubser, "The Ball-court Petroglyph Boulders," 323–44.

20 Stevens Arroyo, *Cave of the Jagua*.

21 Ibid., 238.

22 Ibid., 237.

23 Oliver, "Proto-Taíno Monumental *Cemís*," 251.

24 For pictures of cemís, see https://www.facebook.com/media/set/?set=a.36441 3276905037.96153.142131005799933&type=3] (accessed 17 February 2016).

25 Keegan and Florida Museum, *Taíno Indian Myth and Practice*, 61.

26 Pané and Arrom, *An Account*, 61, 57, 59, 22.

27 Ibid., 21–5.

28 Keegan, *Taíno Indian Myth and Practice*, 69.

29 Oliver, *Caciques and Cemí Idols*, 14.

30 Anderson-Córdoba, "The Aftermath of Conquest," 347–8. The census of 1530 counted only the Taíno living within the Spanish settlements, not people living by themselves in the mountains, who were beyond the reach of the census takers. See Stevens Arroyo, "Indigenous Elements," 105.

31 Stevens Arroyo, "Indigenous Elements," 96; Abbad y Lasierra and Acosta, *Historia geográfica, civil y natural*, 122.

32 Schroeder et al., "Origins and Genetic Legacies."

33 On the debate about Taíno revivalism, see Curet, "Indigenous Revival," 206–47.

34 Stevens Arroyo, *Cave of the Jagua*, 254–5.

35 Oliver, *Caciques and Cemí Idols*, 228.

36 Ibid., 253.

37 Vidal, *Oraciones, conjuros y ensalmo*, 82.

CHAPTER TWO

1 There did not appear to be a hierarchy of caciques in Puerto Rico; rather each exercised power over a given territory. In Spain, of course, the king held sway over the whole kingdom and had military and administrative subordinates in each province.

2 Martínez, "El clero ante la crisis," 2.

3 Ibid.

4 Rawlings, *Church, Religion and Society*, 53.

5 Ibid., 130, 131, 135.

6 Ibid., 12–16.

7 Ibid., 14, 23.

8 Ibid., 38–42.

9 Ibid., 7, 13–24, 26.

10 Stevens Arroyo, "The Inter-Atlantic Paradigm," 515, 520–41.

11 Rawlings, *Church, Religion and Society*, 101.

12 Hanke, *Spanish Struggle for Justice*, 17–24.

13 Ibid., 21.

14 Ibid., 21, 56, 74–5, 87–92, 122–8, 150–3.

15 Ibid., 8–10, 12, 46.

16 Rawlings, *Church, Religion and Society*, 109.

17 Stevens Arroyo, "Indigenous Elements," 96, 99, 100, 109.

18 Rawlings, *Church, Religion and Society*, 65–6.

19 Ibid., 59.

20 Ibid., 69.

21 Ibid., 71.

22 Ibid., 72–3, 77.

23 Deleito y Piñuela, *La vida religiosa española*, 86, 91, 93.

24 Ibid., 91.

25 Ibid., 96.

26 Ibid., 106, 113, 130.

27 Sarrailh, "La crise spirituelle et économique," 5, 12, 13.

28 Peña Díaz, "Tolerar la costumbre," 777–806; López Muñoz, "La fiesta religiosa," 239–78.

29 Christian, *Local Religion in Sixteenth-Century Spain*, 5, 178.

30 Ibid., 44–6.

31 Ibid., 175–6, 31, 125.

32 Ibid., 46.

33 Ibid., 35, 56, 97.

34 Ibid., 75, 46.

35 Ibid., 175.

36 Ibid., 46, 88, 103.

37 Ibid., 182, 186.

38 Arias de Saavedra Alías and López-Guadalupe Muñoz, "Las cofradías," 205, 217, 219, 228.

39 Deleito y Piñuela, *La vida religiosa española*, 186–90.

40　Ibid., 196–200.

41　Rawlings, *Church, Religion and Society*, 93.

42　Deleito y Piñuela, *La vida religiosa española*, 217, 254.

43　Ibid., 239–47.

44　Ibid., 262, 265, 270–4.

45　Rawlings, *Church, Religion and Society*, 80, 84–5.

46　Christian, *Local Religion in Sixteenth-Century Spain*, 167.

47　Rawlings, *Church, Religion and Society*, 80–2.

CHAPTER THREE

1　Scarano, *Puerto Rico*, 124–31.

2　Ibid., 130.

3　Dussel and Comisión de Estudios, *Historia general de la Iglesia*, 349.

4　Meier, "La historia de las diócesis de Santo Domingo," 108.

5　Dussel and Comisión de Estudios, *Historia general de la Iglesia*, 497.

6　Rodríguez León, "Introducción," xxxii.

7　Sued Badillo and López Cantos, *Puerto Rico negro*, 152, 163.

8　Meier, "La historia de las diócesis" 149–51.

9　Rafael L. López Valdés, email, 21 February 2020.

10　Brau, *Ensayos*, 141.

11　Dussel and Comisión de Estudios, *Historia general de la Iglesia*, 622–3.

12　Ibid., 573, 580–90.

13　Ibid., 598–606.

14　Arias de Saavedra Alías and López-Guadalupe Muñoz, "Las cofradías," 189–232.

15　David M. Cheney, "Hierarchy of the Catholic Church," http://www.catholic-hierarchy.org/diocese/dsjpr.html (accessed 1 October 2018).

16　Torres y Vargas, Vidal, and Stevens Arroyo, *Report on the Island & Diocese of Puerto Rico*, 135–53.

17　Campo Lacasa, *Historia de la Iglesia en Puerto Rico*, 214–19.

18　Meier, "La historia de las diócesis," 143.

19　Dussel and Comisión de Estudios, *Historia general*, 467.

20　Cuesta Mendoza, *Historia eclesiástica*, 50.

21　Perea, *Historia de Puerto Rico*, 192.

22 Stevens Arroyo, "Understanding the Work of Diego De Torres y Vargas," 22.

23 Melgarejo, "Memoria y descripción," 88.

24 Stevens Arroyo, "Understanding," 22.

25 Meier, "La historia de las diócesis," 96.

26 Diaz Stevens, *Oxcart Catholicism*, 40.

27 Perea, *Historia de Puerto Rico*, 98–9.

28 Torres y Vargas and Stevens Arroyo, *Report*, 82.

29 Cuesta Mendoza, *Historia eclesiástica*, 218.

30 Ibid., 224.

31 Campo Lacasa, *Historia de la Iglesia*, 53, 104.

32 Ibid., 100, 107, 129–30.

33 Rodríguez León, "Introducción," lxi.

34 Campo Lacasa, *Historia de la Iglesia*, 140, 277.

35 López Cantos, *La religiosidad popular*, 19, 24.

36 Carroll, *Report on the Island of Porto Rico*, 656. The American administration's misspelling of the island's name would continue until Congress formally restored the Spanish spelling in 1932. See https://history.house.gov/Exhibitions-and-Publications/HAIC/Historical-Essays/Foreign-Domestic/Crafting-Identity (accessed 17 December 2020).

37 Campo Lacasa, *Historia de la Iglesia*, 133.

38 López de Haro, *Constituciones sinodales*, 7. Quotations from Spanish-language sources are the author's translations.

39 Campo Lacasa, *Historia de la Iglesia*, 303; López de Haro, *Sínodo de San Juan*, xvi, 62.

40 Campo Lacasa, *Historia de la Iglesia*, 104, 130.

41 López Cantos, *La religiosidad popular*, 10.

42 López de Haro, *Sínodo de San Juan*, 33.

43 Picó, *Historia general*, 176.

44 Campo Lacasa, *Historia de la Iglesia*, 66, 73.

45 Rodríguez León, "Introducción," xxii.

46 Campo Lacasa, *Historia de la Iglesia*, 280.

47 López de Haro, *Sínodo de San Juan*, 53.

48 Campo Lacasa, *Historia de la Iglesia*, 81, 84, 123.

49 Rodríguez León, "Introducción," xxxvii.

50 Ibid., xxxiv, xxxv.

51   Campo Lacasa, *Historia de la Iglesia*, 193.

52   López de Haro, *Sínodo de San Juan*, xl, 66. A *real* was one-eighth of the peso, or Spanish dollar, in which the bishop's salary was denominated. In the eighteenth century, the daily wage for a master mason was eighteen reales. See López Cantos, *La religiosidad popular*, 60. On the history of the peso, see Pond, "The Spanish Dollar."

53   López Cantos, *La religiosidad popular*, 62.

54   Zayas Micheli, *Catolicismo popular*, 42; Meier, "La historia de las diócesis," 50-1.

55   Cuesta Mendoza, *Historia eclesiástica*, 254–5.

56   Diócesis de Mayagüez, "Basílica Ntra. Sra. de la Monserrate," Diócesis de Mayagüez, http://www.diocesisdemayaguez.org/index.php/directorio/parroquias-y-misas/18-basilica-ntra-sra-de-la-monserrate (accessed 16 December 2019).

57   Reichard de Cancio, *Puerto Rico*, 255.

58   López de Haro, *Sínodo de San Juan*, 67.

59   Reichard de Cancio, *Temas y Temitas*, 148–9; López Cantos, *La religiosidad popular*, 40, 42.

60   Abbad y Lasierra and Acosta, *Historia geográfica*, 407–8.

61   Campo Lacasa, *Historia de la Iglesia*, 145–6.

62   Torres y Vargas and Stevens Arroyo, *Report*, 139.

63   Rodríguez León, "Introducción," liii.

64   Torres y Vargas and Stevens Arroyo, *Report*, 211, 213.

65   López de Haro, *Constituciones sinodales*, 91–2.

66   Campo Lacasa, *Historia de la Iglesia*, 81, 108–9.

67   López Cantos, *La religiosidad popular*, 32.

68   Campo Lacasa, *Historia de la Iglesia*, 190.

69   López Cantos, *La religiosidad popular*, 35.

70   Brau, *Historia de Puerto Rico*, 158.

71   Cuesta Mendoza, *Historia eclesiástica*, 285.

72   Campo Lacasa, *Historia de la Iglesia*, 130.

73   Camaño-Dones, "La sociedad colonial," 217, 222–3.

74   López Cantos, *La religiosidad popular*, 21.

CHAPTER FOUR

1 Congreso de los Deputados, "Constitución de 1812," Congreso de los Deputados, http://www.congreso.es/portal/page/portal/Congreso/ Congreso/Hist_Normas/ConstEsp1812_1978/Consti1812 9 (accessed 17 December 2019).
2 Martínez Tornero, *Carlos III y los bienes de los jesuítas*, 162.
3 Callahan, *Church, Politics, and Society in Spain*, 110.
4 Ibid., 113, 116–17, 133, 135.
5 Ibid., 159, 163, 168, 200.
6 Ibid., 218–20, 212.
7 Ibid., 181, 232–5.
8 Ibid., 236–40, 253.
9 Andrés-Gallego and Pazos, *Histoire religieuse de l'Espagne*, 57–8.
10 Callahan, *Church, Politics, and Society in Spain*, 199, 181–2, 174.
11 I take the start of building a church as launching a formal Catholic community. The data in the graph indicate either the start of construction or, if that is not available, the first mention of a parish church. *Ermitas* (chapels) were excluded from the data.
12 Scarano, *Puerto Rico*, 266.
13 Martín Ramos, *Las comunicaciones*, table 1.
14 Ibid., 281, 252.
15 Picó, *Libertad y servidumbre*, 136.
16 García Leduc, *¡La pesada carga!*, 53, 55, 69, 75, 85, 97–8, 109, 115, 124.
17 Carroll, *Report on the Island of Porto Rico*, 22.
18 Hernández García, "Una columna fortísima," 552.
19 García Leduc, *¡La pesada carga!*, 137.
20 Carroll, *Report*, 28.
21 Rodríguez Pérez, "La obra de los Hermanos Cheo," 39, 161, 167.
22 Carroll, *Report*, 29.
23 Ibid., 10.
24 Silva Gotay, *Catolicismo y política*, 240; and *La iglesia católica*, 104.
25 Hamelin, *Le XXe siècle*, 2:124.
26 Cruz Monclova, *Historia de Puerto Rico* [1970], 40.
27 Scarano, *Puerto Rico*, 296–7.
28 Hernández García, "Una columna fortísima," 546.

29 García Leduc, "Proyección social," 23–5.

30 Ortiz Diaz, "La manifestación anticlerical," 176–9.

31 Cruz Monclova, *Historia de Puerto Rico* [1970], 89.

32 García Leduc, "Proyección social," 19.

33 Salcedo Chirinos, "Estragos tropicales de la lujuria," 47–50; Hernández García, "Una columna fortísima," 548.

34 Agosto Cintrón, *Religión y cambio social*, 39–40.

35 Ortiz Diaz, "La manifestación anticlerical," 184.

36 García Leduc, *¡La pesada carga!*, 265.

37 Picó, *Libertad y servidumbre*, 134.

38 Gagnon and Lebel-Gagnon, "Le milieu d'origine du clergé québécois."

39 Connolly, *Priests and People in Pre-Famine Ireland*, 59–69.

40 Picó, *Libertad y servidumbre*, 136.

41 Cruz Monclova, *Historia de Puerto Rico* [1970], 496.

42 Picó, *Libertad y servidumbre*, 136–7.

43 García Leduc, *¡La pesada carga!*, 230.

44 Silva Gotay, *Soldado católico*, 50.

45 Steward, *The People of Puerto Rico*, 60.

46 Picó, "La religiosidad popular," 157.

47 Reichard de Cancio, "Desarollo de la religión popular católica."

48 Duany, "La religiosidad popular," 168.

49 Reichard de Cancio, *Puerto Rico*, 79.

50 Ibid., 126–7.

51 Valle Atiles, *El campesino puertorriqueño*, 127–9.

52 Juan Torres Rivera, "Las Fiestas de Cruz. Letras y midis," http://www.puertadetierra.info/eventos/FdeCrz/fiesta_cruz/fiestas_de_cruz.htm (accessed 30 January 2017).

53 Picó, "La religiosidad popular," 159.

54 Callahan, *Church, Politics, and Society in Spain*, 232.

CHAPTER FIVE

1 Martín Ramos, *Las comunicaciones*, Estadillo no. 1.

2 Ibid., 252–67.

3 Cruz Monclova, *Historia de Puerto Rico* [1970], 69–70.

4 Romero López, "La reducción de la influencia," 54.

5   Wagenheim, *El grito de Lares*, 135.

6   Cruz Monclova, *Historia de Puerto Rico* [1957], 417, 863.

7   Silva Gotay, *Soldado católico*, 84–8.

8   Cruz Monclova, *Historia de Puerto Rico* [1964], 513.

9   Cruz Monclova, *Historia de Puerto Rico* [1970], 112–13, 239, 359.

10 Cruz Monclova, *Historia de Puerto Rico* [1957], 664.

11 Ortiz Diaz, "La manifestación anticlerical," 174, 184.

12 Partsch, *La crisis de 1898*, 22.

13 García Leduc, *¡La pesada carga!*, 246.

14 Romero López, "La reducción de la influencia," 259–63.

15 Cruz Monclova, *Historia de Puerto Rico* [1957], 861, 864.

16 Ibid., 859.

17 Edward Camareno Jr, "Manuel Fernández-Juncos Masonic Hero of Puerto
    Rico," http://srjarchives.tripod.com/1998-09/CAMARENO.HTM (accessed
    20 February 2017); Grupo Editorial EPRL, "Fernández Juncos, Manuel."

18 Silva Gotay, *Soldado católico*, 140.

19 Wagenheim, *El grito de Lares*, 135.

20 Silva Gotay, *Soldado católico*, 131–9, 157–60.

21 Ibid., 114, 119, 123, 125.

22 Callahan, *Church, Politics, and Society in Spain*, 212.

23 Cruz Monclova, *Historia de Puerto Rico* [1970], 364.

24 Callahan, *The Catholic Church in Spain*, 210.

25 Ibid., 260.

26 Ibid., 212, 219.

27 Ibid., 267–70.

28 Jiménez Duque, *La espiritualidad en el siglo XIX*, 145–9.

29 Ibid., 155–7.

30 Cruz Monclova, *Historia de Puerto Rico* [1957], 852.

31 Martínez-Fernández, "Crypto-Protestants and Pseudo-Catholics," 347–65.

32 Silva Gotay, "Puerto Rico," 728.

33 Reichard de Cancio, "Desarrollo."

34 Carroll, *Report on the Island of Porto Rico*, 33, 200.

35 Reichard de Cancio, "Desarrollo."

36 Ayala, "La masoneria de obediencia francesa," 65–82.

37 Ayala, *La masonería de obediencia española*, 15.

38 Ibid.

39 Silva Gotay, *Soldado católico*, 140–2.

40 García Leduc, *Intolerancia y heterodoxias*, 109.

41 Silva Gotay, *Soldado católico*, 141.

42 Ayala, *La masonería de obediencia española*, 277–84, 268, 257, 264–5.

43 Cruz Monclova, *Historia de Puerto Rico* [1957], 860.

44 Ayala, *La masonería de obediencia española*, 32, 152–3, 162, 167, 157.

45 Silva Gotay, *Soldado católico*, 159.

46 Romero López, "La reducción de la influencia," 136.

47 Silva Gotay, *Soldado católico*, 157–9; Romero López, "La reducción de la influencia," 54.

48 Ayala, *La masonería de obediencia española*, 142.

49 Cruz Monclova, *Historia de Puerto Rico* [1964], 336.

50 García Leduc, *Intolerancia y heterodoxias*, 118.

51 Daniel Assisi, "Allan Kardec – The Codifier of Spiritism," http://www.allankardec.org (accessed 4 July 2017).

52 Blackwell, "Translator's Preface," 11–14.

53 Kardec, *Spiritualist Philosophy*, 24.

54 Koss, "El porqué de los cultos religiosos," 66.

55 Koss, "Religion and Science Divinely Related," 31.

56 Koss, "El porqué de los cultos religiosos," 66; Cruz Monclova, *Historia de Puerto Rico* [1957], 855.

57 Koss, "Religion and Science," 31.

58 Fernández Olmos, *Creole Religions of the Caribbean*, 177.

59 Román, *Governing Spirits*, 77.

60 Koss, "El porqué de los cultos religiosos," 68–9.

61 Silva Gotay, *Soldado católico*, 143.

62 Cruz Monclova, *Historia de Puerto Rico* [1957], 855–6.

63 Koss, "El porqué de los cultos religiosos," 68–9.

64 Fernández Olmos, *Creole Religions*, 186–7.

65 Koss, "Religion and Science," 188.

66 Fernández Olmos, *Creole Religions*, 187.

67 Cruz Monclova, *Historia de Puerto Rico* [1957], 861–2.

68 Cruz Monclova, *Historia de Puerto Rico* [1964], 337.

69 Ibid., 334.

70 García Leduc, *Intolerancia y heterodoxias*.

71 Ortiz Diaz, "La manifestación anticlerical."

CHAPTER SIX

1 Carroll, *Report on the Island of Porto Rico*, 7–8, 63–4, 31.
2 Silva Gotay, *La iglesia católica de Puerto Rico*, 69.
3 Carroll, *Report*, 65.
4 Silva Gotay, *La iglesia católica*, 78, 242.
5 Clark et al., *Porto Rico and Its Problems*, 72.
6 Silva Gotay, *La iglesia católica*, 129.
7 Partsch, *La crisis de 1898*, 59.
8 Silva Gotay, *La iglesia católica*, 101.
9 Romero López, "La reducción de la influencia," 246; Partsch, *La crisis*, 98.
10 Partsch, *La crisis*, 60–1, 50, 10, 81, 71, 74.
11 Silva Gotay, *La iglesia católica*, 188.
12 Stevens Arroyo, "Pious Colonialism," 57–82.
13 Silva Gotay, *La iglesia católica*, 323–4.
14 Ibid., 152.
15 Ibid., 219–21.
16 Pérez Rivera, "La Asociación de Católicos de Ponce," 55–70.
17 Silva Gotay, *La iglesia católica*, 217.
18 Ibid., 104.
19 Partsch, *La crisis*, 81–2, 157.
20 Silva Gotay, *La iglesia católica*, 166, 161.
21 Partsch, *La crisis*, 95.
22 Ibid., 104, 139.
23 Silva Gotay, *La iglesia católica*, 227.
24 Ibid., 165.
25 Ibid., 168.
26 Ibid., 169–73.
27 Partsch, *La crisis*, 139.
28 Silva Gotay, *La iglesia católica*, 165; Partsch, *La crisis*, 129.
29 Silva Gotay, *La iglesia católica*, 300.
30 Ibid., 120–1, 134, 139, 135, 210.
31 Columbia University Teachers College and University of Puerto Rico, *A Survey of the Public Educational System*, 23–4.
32 Partsch, *La crisis*, 115–17.
33 Silva Gotay, *La iglesia católica*, 144, 272.

34 Ibid., 274, 271.

35 Columbia University Teachers College and University of Puerto Rico, *Survey*, 21.

36 Silva Gotay, *La iglesia católica*, 289.

37 Partsch, *La crisis*, 146.

38 Jones, *Sínodo diocesano*, 39.

39 Pérez Rivera, "La Asociación," 60–2.

40 Jones, *Sínodo diocesano*, 37; Reichard de Cancio, *Puerto Rico*, 149.

41 Fenton, *Understanding the Religious Background of the Puerto Rican*, 2: 4.

42 Herzig Shannon, *El Iris de Paz*, 89–90.

43 Silva Gotay, *La iglesia católica*, 118, 155, 125.

44 Rodríguez Escudero, *Historia del espiritismo*, 6–7.

45 Herzig Shannon, *El Iris de Paz*, 72.

46 Ibid., 107, 49, 92.

47 Agosto Cintrón, *Religión y cambio social*, 43.

48 Román, *Governing Spirits*, 112.

49 Ibid., 114, 116; see also Román, "Spiritists versus Spirit-mongers."

50 Román, *Governing Spirits*, 113, 115.

51 Koss, "Religion and Science Divinely Related," 37–8.

52 Agosto Cintrón, *Religión y cambio social*, 12.

53 Silva Gotay, *La iglesia católica*, 179.

54 Román, *Governing Spirits*, 78.

55 Santaella Rivera, *Historia de los Hermanos Cheos*, 49.

56 Reichard de Cancio, "Desarollo de la religión popular católica"; Silva Gotay, *La iglesia católica*, 175–8.

57 Rodríguez Pérez, "La obra de los Hermanos Cheo," 64–6.

58 Santaella Rivera, *Historia*, 56.

59 Román, *Governing Spirits*, 78, 54.

60 Rodríguez Pérez, "La obra," 71–2; Santaella Rivera, *Historia*, 77–83.

61 Silva Gotay, *La iglesia católica*, 178.

62 Rodríguez Pérez, "La obra," 118, 92.

63 Agosto Cintrón, *Religión*, 79.

64 Rodríguez Pérez, "La obra," 131–2.

65 Silva Gotay, *La iglesia católica*, 181–4.

66 Agosto Cintrón, *Religión*, 61, 74, 77, 80.

67 Román, *Governing Spirits*, 54.

68 Agosto Cintrón, *Religión*, 80.

69 "Mystical Mountain in San Lorenzo," *El Nuevo Día*, 30 March 2012; Rodríguez Pérez, "La obra," 68, 133; Congregación misionera de San Juan Evan-
gelista Hermanos Cheos, "Consagración a María en la Montaña Santa
en San Lorenzo, PR 2010," http://www.hermanoscheos.org/consagracio
acuten-a-mariacutea-en-la-montantildea-santa-en-san-lorenzo-pr-2010
.html (accessed 24 October 2017).

70 Santaella Rivera, *Historia*, 163.

71 Rodríguez Pérez, "La obra," 74, 72, 77, 75.

72 Ibid., 77–8, 156–7, 170; Román, *Governing Spirits*, 78–9.

73 Santaella Rivera, *Historia*, 161–2.

74 Reichard de Cancio, "Desarollo."

CHAPTER SEVEN

1 Silva Gotay, *Protestantismo y política*, 112–14; Macfee, "To-day in Porto
Rico," 583.

2 Silva Gotay, *Protestantismo*, 112–14.

3 Ibid., 116–19.

4 Ibid., 120.

5 Ibid., 121–2.

6 Ibid., 123–7.

7 Ibid., 128.

8 Ibid., 131–3.

9 Ibid., 134–7.

10 Ibid., 144–5.

11 Agosto Cintrón, *Religión y cambio social*, 137.

12 Silva Gotay, *Protestantismo*, 150–65.

13 Ibid., 174, 149.

14 Linde and Friend, "Victor S. Clark Papers."

15 Silva Gotay, *Protestantismo*, 200, 246.

16 Díaz Stevens, "Aspects of the Puerto Rican Religious Experience," 160.

17 Negrón de Montilla, *Americanization in Puerto Rico*, 121–2.

18 Silva Gotay, *Protestantismo*, 184–5.

19 Ibid., 214.

20 Ibid., 232, 259.

21 Ibid., 234.

22 Ibid., 228.

23 Ibid., 175, 234.

24 Ibid., 196, 209–10.

25 Ibid., 183–7.

26 United States, Bureau of the Census, *Fifteenth Census of the United States: 1930. Population*, 1:1251.

27 Silva Gotay, *Protestantismo*, 257; Universidad de Puerto Rico, "Historia de la UPR," http://www.upr.edu/historia/ (accessed 7 December 2017).

28 Agosto Cintrón, *Religión*, 38, 114.

29 Manners, "Tabara," 127.

30 Silva Gotay, *Protestantismo*, 260, 263.

31 Agosto Cintrón, *Religión*, 13–14, 99–114.

32 Mintz, *Worker in the Cane*, 248.

33 Ibid., 211–24.

34 Ibid., 216, 250, 264.

35 Ibid., 266.

36 Agosto Cintrón, *Religión*, 105.

37 Mintz, "Cañamelar," 409.

38 Agosto Cintrón, *Religión*, 107, 152–5; Rogler, *Comerío*, 133, 135.

39 Rogler, *Comerío*, 139, 142.

40 Ibid., 134.

41 Ibid., 133.

42 Manners, "Tabara," 127.

CHAPTER EIGHT

1 Coleson, "La puertorriqueñización del protestantismo," 41.

2 Padilla Seda, "Nocorá," 303.

3 Martin, *Tongues of Fire*, 58.

4 Steward, *The People of Puerto Rico*, 85, 475.

5 Rogler, *Comerío*, 131.

6 Silva Gotay, *La iglesia católica de Puerto Rico*, 174.

7 Fenton, *Understanding the Religious Background of the Puerto Rican*, 2:4.

8 Loebach, "Problems," 2:2.

9 Wipfler, "La Iglesia católica y la dictadura de Trujillo," 369.

10 Hamelin, *Le XXe siècle*, 2:162.

11 Silva Gotay, *La iglesia católica*, 318.

12 Loebach, "Problems," 2:2.

13 Mintz, "Puerto Rico," 424.

14 Reichard de Cancio, *Puerto Rico*, 198.

15 Duany, "La religiosidad popular," 165.

16 Hamelin, *Le XXe siècle*, 2:109–89.

17 Rogler, *Comerío*, 138, 140–1, 32.

18 Ibid., 81–2, 20, 66.

19 Ibid., 73–5, 77, 90.

20 Ibid., 157, 35, 158, 147–8.

21 Agosto Cintrón, *Religión y cambio social*, 87.

22 Fenton, *Understanding*, 2:6, 8.

23 Hatt, *Backgrounds of Human Fertility*, 41, 38.

24 Ibid., 29, 200, 260, 47, 79.

25 Silverman, "Introduction," 181.

26 Manners, "Tabara," 126; Wolf, "San José," 242; Mintz, "Cañamelar," 406; Padilla Seda, "Nocorá," 303, 305.

27 Manners, "Tabara," 126–9, 149–50.

28 Wolf, "San José," 242–4, 214–15, 245.

29 Padilla Seda, "Nocorá," 303–8.

30 Mintz, "Cañamelar," 406–9; Mintz, *Worker in the Cane*, 247.

31 Baselga, "Cultural Change and Protestantism," 113, 116.

32 Fenton, *Understanding*, 2:6–8.

33 Reichard de Cancio, *Puerto Rico*, 168–9.

34 Fenton, *Understanding*, 2:9.

35 Garrido, *Esoteria y fervor populares*, 43–195, 219, 38.

36 Vidal, *Oraciones, conjuros y ensalmo*, 72–82.

37 Deleito y Piñuela, *La vida religiosa española*, 273–4.

38 Garrido, *Esoteria*, 79.

39 Davila, "Santuario de la Monserrate de Hormigueros," 3.

40 Diaz Stevens, *Oxcart Catholicism*, 6–8.

41 Tumin and Feldman, "The Miracle at Sabana Grande," 355–7, 366, 361, 363.

42 Román, *Governing Spirits*, 166, 168.

43 Tumin and Feldman, "Miracle," 359–61.

44 Ibid., 366.

45 Román, *Governing Spirits*, 175.

46 LaRuffa, *San Cipriano*, 73, 29, 89.

47 Baselga, "Cultural Change and Protestantism," 114, 133–5.

48 Loebach, "Problems," 2:3–4.

49 Stevens Arroyo, "The Catholic Worldview," 53–73; Buxeda Díaz, "Iglesias y modernidad," 130.

50 Zayas Micheli, *Catolicismo popular*, 190, 197.

51 Silva Gotay, *Catolicismo y política*, 424–5.

52 Silva Gotay, *La iglesia católica*, 290–1.

53 Buxeda Díaz, "Iglesias y modernidad," 167–8.

54 Malavet, *America's Colony*, 44.

55 Archivo de las Elecciones en Puerto Rico, "Escrutinio de las Elecciones Generales del 4 de noviembre de 1952: Resultados para candidatos a gobernador del Estado Libre Asociado de Puerto Rico," http://electionspuertori co.org/archivo/1952.html (accessed 15 October 2018).

56 Zayas Micheli, *Catolicismo popular*, 124–5.

57 Ocampo, *Puerto Rico*, 4:37.

58 Archivo de las Elecciones en Puerto Rico, "Escrutinio de las Elecciones Generales del 4 de noviembre de 1960: Resultados para Candidatos a Gobernador del Estado Libre Asociado de Puerto Rico," http://electionspuer-torico.org/archivo/1960.html (accessed 15 October 2018).

59 Zayas Micheli, *Catolicismo popular*, 128.

60 Laboy Gómez, *Los católicos rebeldes*; Silva Gotay, *El pensamiento cristiano revolucionario*.

61 Díaz Stevens, "La Misa Jíbara," 149.

62 For a recent celebration of the *Misa Jíbara*, see https://www.youtube.com/watch?v=agvqrdWNsNo (accessed 3 October 2018).

63 Díaz Stevens, "La Misa Jíbara," 153.

64 Ibid., 152–5.

65 Stevens Arroyo, "The Catholic Worldview," 73.

66 Santiago Santana, *Antulio Parrilla Bonilla*, 25–44.

67 Ibid., 53–5.

68 Ibid., 56–72.

69 Ibid., 63, 362, 377–407, 360, 410, 415.

70 Ibid., 343–7; Silva Gotay, "Desarrollo de la dimensión religiosa del nacionalismo."

71 Laboy Gómez, *Los católicos rebeldes*, 98–188.

72 Ibid., 189–98.

73 Ibid., 229–310.

74 Díaz Stevens, "La Misa Jíbara," 157.

75 Ibid., 156.

76 Laboy Gómez, *Los católicos rebeldes*, 241–3, 220, 291–2, 232.

77 Silva Gotay, "Desarrollo."

78 Buxeda Díaz, "Iglesias," 196, 202.

79 Sáez, *Entre Cristo y Che Guevara*, 35, 41, 143.

80 Silva Gotay, *El pensamiento cristiano revolucionario*; Luis Rivera Pagán, "Samuel Silva Gotay: Un doctorado honoris causa muy merecido," https://mgrafias.wordpress.com/2014/06/04/samuel-silva-gotay-un-doctorado-honoris-causa-muy-merecido (accessed 4 May 2018).

CHAPTER NINE

1 PROLADES, RITA Database of Puerto Rico, http://prolades.com/cra/regions/caribe/pri/rita_dbase_prico.htm (accessed 10 October 2018).

2 Bell and Sahgal, *Religion in Latin America*, 4.

3 Scott Cook, "The Prophets," 20.

4 Bastian, "Metamorphosis," 41.

5 Clifton L. Holland, *Table of Estimated Size of the Protestant Movement in Puerto Rico, 2000*, http://prolades.com/cra/regions/caribe/pri/pri-tbl-prot_2000.pdf (accessed 28 May 2018).

6 Bell and Sahgal, *Religion in Latin America*, 14.

7 Uribe, *Les transformations du christianisme*, 93, 120, 189, 172.

8 Bell and Sahgal, *Religion in Latin America*, 8.

9 My calculations of Bell and Sahgal, Religion in Latin America Dataset. Variables QPROT, Q28a, Q28a by QPOT.

10 Martin, *Tongues of Fire*, 282, 133.

11 Agosto Cintrón, *Religión y cambio social*, 105, 111.

12 Ibid., 98.

13 LaRuffa, *San Cipriano*, 142, 129.

14 Baselga, "Cultural Change and Protestantism," 182.

15 Bell and Sahgal, Religion in Latin America Dataset, QCURRELrec by Q73.

16 Bell and Sahgal, *Religion in Latin America*, 42.

17 Bell and Sahgal, Religion in Latin America Dataset, Q67a by Q73 by
    QCURRELrec.

18 Ibid., Q58 by Q73.

19 Bell and Sahgal, *Religion in Latin America*, 31, 34, 38, 49.

20 Uribe, *Les transformations*, 160.

21 Duany, "La religiosidad popular," 174.

22 Fenton, *Understanding the Religious Background of the Puerto Rican*, 3:6.

23 LaRuffa, *San Cipriano*, 105.

24 Fenton, *Understanding*, 3:15.

25 LaRuffa, "Pentecostalism," 51.

26 LaRuffa, *San Cipriano*, 114–15, 118–19, 106.

27 Ibid., 104–6.

28 Scott Cook, "The Prophets," 21, 30.

29 Ibid., 21, 27, 24–5, 30.

30 Ibid., 25.

31 Jewish Virtual Library, "Puerto Rico Virtual Jewish History Tour," Ameri-
    can-Israeli Cooperative Enterprise, http://www.jewishvirtuallibrary.org
    /puerto-rico-virtual-jewish-history-tour (accessed 16 November 2017);
    interview with Diego Mendelbaum.

32 Museo de San Juan, *Los Judios en Puerto Rico/Jews in Puerto Rico*, 10–11.

33 Harry A. Ezratti, "Crypto Jews in Puerto Rico Welcomed by Reform Com-
    munity," Society for Crypto Judaic Studies, https://cryptojews.com/2018/07/
    crypto-jews-in-puerto-rico-welcomed-by-reform-community (accessed
    29 December 2019).

34 Fernando Picó, "Rastros rayados."

35 Museo de San Juan, *Jews in Puerto Rico*, 11–12.

36 Yvette Alt Miller, "Jews and Puerto Rico: 7 Facts," http://www.aish.com
    /jw/s/Jews-and-Puerto-Rico-7-Facts.html (accessed 16 November 2017).

37 Ursula Acosta, "The Brugman Family: Translation of an Excerpt from
    'Puerto Rico y Curazao,'" http://home.coqui.net/uahorm/brugman.html
    (accessed 23 February 2015).

38 Museo de San Juan, *Jews in Puerto Rico*, 14.

39 Miller, "Jews and Puerto Rico: 7 Facts"; Museo de San Juan, *Jews in Puerto
    Rico*, 14–15.

40 Museo de San Juan, *Jews in Puerto Rico*, 22–5, 17.

41 Román Vádiz, "The Development of the Jewish Community," 51, 69–70, 74.

42 Museo de San Juan, *Jews in Puerto Rico*, 34–5, 41.

43 Ibid., 43, 48; interview with Diego Mendelbaum.

44 Museo de San Juan, *Jews in Puerto Rico*, 56–65.

45 Interview with Diego Mendelbaum.

46 Museo de San Juan, *Jews in Puerto Rico*, 66–7; Temple Beth Shalom, "The Beginning of Our Synagogue," https://tbspr.org/beginnings (accessed 12 February 2019).

47 "Welcome, Shalom, Bienvenidos," https://tbspr.org/about (accessed 12 February 2019).

48 Interview with Rabbi Norman Patz.

49 Chabad.org, "Chabad Lubavitch of Puerto Rico – Carolina, Puerto Rico," https://www.chabad.org/centers/default_cdo/aid/118318/jewish/Chabad-Lubavitch-of-Puerto-Rico.htm (accessed 28 May 2018); Zarchi, "About Us – Chabad of Puerto Rico," http://www.chabadpr.com (accessed 28 May 2018).

50 Chabad of Puerto Rico, "Construction Update – Chabad of Puerto Rico Building Campaign," Chabad of Puerto Rico, https://www.caribbeanjewish center.com/construction-updates (accessed 12 March 2019).

51 Interview with Rabbi Mendel Zarchi.

52 Ibid.

53 Patz, "In Memory of the Six Million," 23–5.

54 Chitwood, "On Eid 2017, a Peek into the Lives of Puerto Rican Muslims," Shia News Association, http://en.shafaqna.com/on-eid-2017-a-peek-into-the-lives-of-puerto-rican-muslims (accessed 25 February 2019). See also Karoline P. Cook, *Forbidden Passages*.

55 Ramadan-Santiago, "Introduction of Islam," 1–5.

56 "Del oriente al Caribe: Árabes han hecho de Borinquen su hogar desde finales del siglo XIX," *El Nuevo Día*, 8 November 2013.

57 "Boricuas en el islam," *El Nuevo Día*, 27 September 2008.

58 Houssain Kettani, "Muslims in Puerto Rico | Arab News," http://www.arab news.com/muslims-puerto-rico (accessed 13 March 2015).

59 "Del oriente al Caribe: Árabes han hecho de Borinquen su hogar desde finales del siglo XIX," *El Nuevo Día*, 8 November 2013.

60 Lavarado León, Gerardo E. "Comunidad musulmana en Puerto Rico es la más grande del Caribe," *Islam España*, 7 December 2015.

61 Houssain Kettani, "Muslims in Puerto Rico."

62 Muslimah Boricua, "A Database of Islamic Centers and Masajid in Puerto

Rico," https://muslimahpr.wordpress.com/2010/08/14/a-database-of-islamic-centers-and-masajid-in-puerto-rico (25 February 2019).

63 Houssain Kettani, "Muslims in Puerto Rico."

64 Lavarado León, "Comunidad musulmana en Puerto Rico."

65 Interview with Imam Nabil El Fallah; interview with Imam Yunus Fasasi.

66 Salatomatic, "Salatomatic: The Most Comprehensive Guide to Mosques and Islamic Schools," https://www.salatomatic.com/reg/1sRmJKDkj5 (accessed 25 February 2019).

67 Interview with Juan F. Caraballo Resto.

68 Interview with Imam Nabil El Fallah.

69 Ibid.; interview with Imam Yunus Fasasi.

70 Juan F. Caraballo Resto, *Islam in the Caribbean, or Caribbean Islam: Is There a Difference?*, podcast audio, 2:04:32, https://www.youtube.com/watch?v=bznsXQydYac&list=PLbZeolDzN_Qe00xCNO4aPCxR__XNEpL_H&index=3&t=0s (accessed 12 April 2019).

71 "Boricuas en el islam," *El Nuevo Día*, 27 September 2008.

CHAPTER TEN

1 Julián de Nieves, *The Catholic Church in Colonial Puerto Rico*, 1–2.

2 Zayas Micheli, *Catolicismo popular*, 12, 79.

3 Uribe, *Les transformations du christianisme*, 168.

4 Duany, "La religiosidad popular," 171.

5 Alvarez, "The Puerto Rican Family," 2:16.

6 Loebach, "Problems," 2:3.

7 Zayas Micheli, *Catolicismo popular*, 112.

8 Reichard de Cancio, *Puerto Rico*, 267, 272–4.

9 Reichard de Cancio, *Temas y Temitas*, 151.

10 Valle Ferrer, *Fiestas de Cruz*, 18–19, 21–2.

11 Zaragoza, "The Santiago Apóstol of Loíza," 125–30.

12 Hernández Hiraldo, *Black Puerto Rican Identity*, 43, 110–11.

13 Robles Álvarez, *La marejada de los muertos*, 14, 39.

14 Reichard de Cancio, *Puerto Rico*, 162, and *Temas y Temitas*, 147.

15 Diaz Stevens, *Oxcart Catholicism*, 47–8.

16 Stevens Arroyo, "The Inter-Atlantic Paradigm," 539.

17 Reichard de Cancio, *Puerto Rico*, 256.

18 Ibid., 149.

19 Montes Mock, "Radio religiosa," 47–8, 51, 61, 78, 94, 108, 124, 135, 231.

20 Stiening, "Streaming Radio Stations by State," at https://streamingradio guide.com/radio-station-list-by-state.php?state=pr (accessed 16 October 2018).

21 Streema, "Puerto Rico TV Stations," https://streema.com/tv/country/ Puerto_Rico (accessed 16 October 2018).

22 Enrique Vargas, "Podcasting in Puerto Rico: pasado, presente y futuro," Centro – Center for Puerto Rican Studies Hunter College CUNY, https:// centropr.hunter.cuny.edu/centrovoices/current-affairs/podcasting-en-puerto-rico-pasado-presente-y-futuro (accessed 5 April 2019).

23 López Sierra, "Construcción," 205.

24 Duany, "La religiosidad popular," 180.

25 López Sierra, "Construcción," 206.

26 Pérez, *Estudio etnográfico de la santería afro-cubana*, 5–10.

27 Mitchell, *Crucial Issues in Caribbean Religions*, 132.

28 "Botánicas/Esoterismo, tiendas de," Directorio de PR.com, https://www.di rectoriodepr.com/categorias/categ-botanica.html (accessed 9 August 2018).

29 "Botanica," SuperPagesPR.com, http://superpagespr.com/Searchpg.aspx? nombre=Bot%C3%A1nica (accessed 9 August 2018).

30 Vidal, *Tradiciones*, xii–xiii, 3, 27–39, 157–63.

31 Sanchez, "Examination"; Jessica Ríos Viner, "Las curanderas: sanadoras en peligro de extinción," *El Nuevo Día*, 2 April 2017.

32 Fenton, *Understanding the Religious Background of the Puerto Rican*, 2:9.

33 Koss, "Religion and Science Divinely Related," 43.

34 Fernández Olmos, *Creole Religions of the Caribbean*, 186–7.

35 Steward, *The People of Puerto Rico*, 88.

36 Padilla Seda, "Nocorá," 303, 306.

37 Wolf, "San José," 245.

38 Garrido, *Esoteria y fervor populares*, 38.

39 Seda, *Social Change and Personality*, xxv, 46, 135.

40 Ibid., 140, 146.

41 Duany, "La religiosidad popular," 176.

42 Harwood, *Rx: Spiritist as Needed*, 28, 30.

43 Ibid., 55.

44 Ibid., 183–4.

45 Ibid., 51.

46 LaRuffa, *San Cipriano*, 80–3.

CONCLUSION

1 Hernández Hiraldo, *Black Puerto Rican Identity*, 121.

2 Alex Figueroa Cancel, "Tribunal reconoce complejidad del caso de quiebra de la Arquidiócesis de San Juan," *El Nuevo Día*, 1 March 2019.

3 Keila López Alicea, "Los jóvenes boricuas cambian las maneras de vivir la fe," *El Nuevo Día*, 19 April 2019.

4 WGSN, "La transformación de la fe," *El Nuevo Día*, 21 April 2019.

5 Marga Parés Arroyo, "Católicos mantienen viva la devoción en la Semana Santa," *El Nuevo Día*, 20 April 2019.

6 Agencia EFE, "Las procesiones de Semana Santa se mantienen vivas en Puerto Rico," *El Nuevo Día*, 10 April 2019.

7 "La Policía arresta a 428 personas en la Semana Santa por embriaguez y droga," *El Nuevo Día*, 22 April 2019.

8 Klein, *The Battle for Paradise*, 65–78.

Bibliography

Abbad y Lasierra, Iñigo, and José J. Acosta. *Historia geográfica, civil y natural de la Isla de San Juan Bautista de Puerto Rico*. San Juan, PR: Imp. y Librería de Acosta, 1866.

Agosto Cintrón, Nélida. *Religión y cambio social en Puerto Rico: 1898–1940*. Río Piedras, PR: Ediciones Huracán; Ateneo Puertorriqueño, 1996.

Alvarez, Wadi. "The Puerto Rican Family." In *Spiritual Care of Puerto Rican Migrants*, ed. William Ferree, Ivan Illich, and Joseph P. Fitzpatrick, part 2, 13–16. New York: Arno Press, 1980.

Anderson, Benedict. *Imagined Communities: Reflections on the Origin and Spread of Nationalism*. London: Verso, 1991.

Anderson-Córdoba, Karen F. "The Aftermath of Conquest: The Indians of Puerto Rico during the Early Sixteenth Century." In *Ancient Borinquen: Archaeology and Ethnohistory of Native Puerto Rico*, ed. Peter E. Siegel, 337–52. Tuscaloosa: University of Alabama Press, 2005.

Andrés-Gallego, José, and Anton Pazos. *Histoire religieuse de l'Espagne*. Paris: Cerf, 1998.

Arias de Saavedra Alías, Inmaculada, and Miguel Luis López-Guadalupe Muñoz. "Las cofradías y su dimensión social en la España del Antiguo Régimen." *Cuadernos de Historia Moderna* 25 (2000): 189–232.

Ayala, José Antonio. *La masonería de obediencia española en Puerto Rico, en el siglo XIX*. Murcia: Universidad de Murcia, 1991.

– *La masonería de obediencia española en Puerto Rico, en el siglo XX*. Murcia: Universidad de Murcia, 1993.

– "La masoneria de obediencia francesa en Puerto Rico de 1821 a 1841." *Cuadernos hispanoamericos* no. 491 (1995): 65–82.

Baselga, Edward M. "Cultural Change and Protestantism in Puerto Rico, 1945–1966." PhD dissertation, New York University, 1971.

Bastian, Jean-Pierre. "The Metamorphosis of Latin American Protestant Groups." *Latin American Research Review* 28, no. 2 (1993): 33–61.

Bell, James, and Neha Sahgal. *Religion in Latin America: Widespread Change in a Historically Catholic Region*. Religion & Public Life. Washington, DC: Pew Research Center, 2014.

– Religion in Latin America: Widespread Change in a Historically Catholic Region Dataset. Washington, DC, 2014. https://www.pewforum.org/dataset/religion-in-latin-america.

Blackwell, Anna. "Translator's Preface." In *Spiritualist Philosophy. The Spirits' Book, containing the principles of Spiritist Doctrine*, 9–19. Boston: Colby and Rich, 1893.

Brau, Salvador. *Ensayos: (disquisiciones sociologicas)*. Rio Piedras, PR: Edil, 1972.

– *Historia de Puerto Rico*. Río Piedras, PR: Editorial Edil, 1974.

Buxeda Díaz, Iván R. "Iglesias y modernidad en Puerto Rico: Conflictos entre la Iglesia Católica Romana y Protestante." PhD dissertation, Universidad de Puerto Rico, 2009.

Callahan, William James. *The Catholic Church in Spain 1875–1998*. Washington, DC: Catholic University of America Press, 2000.

– *Church, Politics, and Society in Spain, 1750–1874*. Cambridge, MA: Harvard University Press, 1984.

Camaño-Dones, Josué. "La sociedad colonial." In *Historia de Puerto Rico*, ed. Luis E. González Vales and Maria Dolores Luque. Historia de las Antillas. San Juan, PR: Consejo superior de investigaciones científicas; Oficina de servicios legislativos, historiador de Puerto Rico; Centro de investigaciones históricas de la UPR, recinto de Río Piedras; Ediciones Doce Calles, 2010.

Campo Lacasa, Cristina. *Historia de la Iglesia en Puerto Rico, 1511–1802*. San Juan, PR: Instituto de Cultura Puertorriquena, 1977.

Caraballo Resto, Juan F. Interview by the author with Juan F. Caraballo Resto, 11 April 2019.

– *Islam in the Caribbean, or Caribbean Islam: Is There a Difference?* Podcast audio 2:04:32. Accessed 12 April 2019. https://www.youtube.com/watch?v= bznsXQydYac&list=PLbZeolDzN_Qeo0xCNO4aPCxR__XNEpL_H&index= 3&t=0s.

Carroll, Henry K. *Report on the Island of Porto Rico; Its Population, Civil Government, Commerce, Industries, Productions, Roads, Tariff, and Currency, with Recommendations.* Washington, DC: Government Printing Office, 1899.

Christian, William A. *Local Religion in Sixteenth-Century Spain.* Princeton, NJ: Princeton University Press, 1981.

Clark, Victor S., et al. *Porto Rico and Its Problems.* Washington, DC: The Brookings Institution, 1930.

Coleson, Jeanene M. "La puertorriqueñización del protestantismo en Puerto Rico, 1898–1939." PhD dissertation, Universidad de Puerto Rico, 2007.

Columbia University Teachers College International Institute, and University of Puerto Rico. *A Survey of the Public Educational System of Porto Rico.* Studies of the International Institute of Teachers College, Columbia University. New York: Teachers College, Columbia University, 1926.

Connolly, S.J. *Priests and People in Pre-Famine Ireland, 1780–1845.* New York: St Martin's Press, 1982.

Cook, Karoline P. *Forbidden Passages: Muslims and Moriscos in Colonial Spanish America.* Philadelphia: University of Pennsylvania Press, 2016.

Cook, Scott. "The Prophets: A Revivalistic Folk Religious Movement in Puerto Rico." *Caribbean Studies* 4, no. 4 (1965): 20–35.

Cruz Monclova, Lidio. *Historia de Puerto Rico (siglo XIX).* 3 vols. Vol. 2, part 2. Río Piedras, PR: Editorial Universitaria, Universidad de Puerto Rico, 1957.

– *Historia de Puerto Rico (siglo XIX).* Vol. 3, part 3. Río Piedras, PR: Editorial Universitaria, Universidad de Puerto Rico, 1964.

– *Historia de Puerto Rico (siglo XIX).* 6th ed. Vol. 1. Río Piedras, PR: Editorial Universitaria, Universidad de Puerto Rico, 1970.

Cuesta Mendoza, Antonio. *Historia eclesiástica del Puerto Rico colonial (1508–1700), Volumen I.* CIDOC-2529. Ciudad Trujillo, Republica Dominicana: Impr. "Arte y Cine," 1948.

Curet, L. Antonio. "Indigenous Revival, Indigeneity, and the Jíbaro in Borikén." *Centro Journal* 27, no. 1 (spring 2015): 206–47.

Curet, L. Antonio, and Lisa M. Stringer. *Tibes Indigenous Ceremonial Center*. S.l., 2010.

Davila, Arturo V. "Santuario de la Monserrate de Hormigueros and Casa de Peregrines, National Register of Historic Place Inventory Nomination Form," ed. National Park Service, 5. Washington, DC: United States Department of the Interior, 1975.

Deleito y Piñuela, José. *La vida religiosa española bajo el cuarto Felipe: santos y pecadores*. Madrid: Espasa-Calpe, 1952.

Díaz Stevens, Ana María. "Aspects of the Puerto Rican Religious Experience: A Sociohistorical Overview." In *Latinos in New York: Communities in Transition*, ed. Gabriel Haslip Viera and Sherrie L. Baver, 147–86. Notre Dame, IN: University of Notre Dame Press, 1996.

– "La Misa Jíbara como campo de batalla sociopolítica en Puerto Rico." *Revista de Ciencias Sociales* 30, no. 1–2 (1993): 139–61.

– *Oxcart Catholicism on Fifth Avenue: The Impact of the Puerto Rican Migration upon the Archdiocese of New York*. Notre Dame, IN: University of Notre Dame Press, 1993.

Duany, Jorge. "La religiosidad popular en Puerto Rico: Reseña de la literatura desde la perspectiva antropologica." In *Virgenes, magos y escapularios*, ed. Angel G. Quintero Rivera, 163–86. San Juan, PR: Centro de Investigaciones Sociales, 1998.

Dussel, Enrique D., and Comisión de Estudios de Historia de la Iglesia en Latinoamérica. *Historia general de la Iglesia en América Latina*. Salamanca: CEHILA; Ediciones Sígueme, 1981.

El Fallah, Nabil. Interview by the author with Imam Nabil El Fallah, Montehiedra mosque, 15 February 2019.

Fasasi, Yunus. Interview by the author by phone with Imam Yunus Fasasi, Vega Alta Islamic Center, 23 February 2019.

Fenton, Jerry. *Understanding the Religious Background of the Puerto Rican*. Cuernavaca, Mexico: Centro Intercultural de Documentacion, 1969.

Fernández Olmos, Margarite. *Creole Religions of the Caribbean: An Introduction from Vodou and Santería to Obeah and Espiritismo*. Religion, Race, and Ethnicity. New York: New York University Press, 2003.

Gagnon, Serge, and Louise Lebel-Gagnon. "Le milieu d'origine du clergé québécois 1775-1840: mythes et réalités." *Revue d'histoire de l'Amérique française* 37, no. 3 (1983): 373–97.

García Leduc, José Manuel. *Intolerancia y heterodoxias en Puerto Rico (siglo XIX): protestantes, masones y espiritistas-kardecianos reclaman su espacio social (cc. 1869–1898). Visiones y cegueras.* San Juan, PR: Isla Negra Editores, 2009.

– *¡La pesada carga!: Iglesia, clero y sociedad en Puerto Rico (siglo XIX): aspectos de su historia.* San Juan, PR: Ediciones Puerto, 2009.

– "Proyección social, política y económica de la Iglesia y el clero católico de Puerto Rico en la primera mitad del sigle XIX: aspectos sobresalientes." In *Tras la huellas del pasado*, ed. Pablo García Colón et al., 11–37. San Juan/Humacao, PR: Editorial Isla Negra/Decanato de Asuntos Académicos, Recinto de Humacao, Universidad de Puerto Rico, 2000.

Garrido, Pablo. *Esoteria y fervor populares de Puerto Rico: contribución al estudio y análisis de la conducta mística del pueblo en sus aspectos intuitivos, tradicionales y vulgares, con una selección de testimonios y experiencias que comprende más de 500 fichas o datos, 16 ilustraciones, 32 melodías y un Mapa Esquemático de Puerto Rico.* Madrid: Ediciones Cultura Hispánica, 1952.

Grupo Editorial EPRL. "Fernández Juncos, Manuel." In *Enciclopedia de Puerto Rico.* San Juan, PR: Fundación Puertorriqueña de las Humanidades, 2014.

Hamelin, Jean. *Le XXe siècle. Histoire du catholicisme québécois.* Vol. 2. Montreal: Boréal Express, 1984.

Hanke, Lewis. *The Spanish Struggle for Justice in the Conquest of America.* Boston, MA: Little, Brown, 2015.

Harwood, Alan. *Rx, Spiritist as Needed: A Study of a Puerto Rican Community Mental Health Resource.* Ithaca, NY: Cornell University Press, 1987.

Hatt, Paul K. *Backgrounds of Human Fertility in Puerto Rico: A Sociological Survey.* Princeton, NJ: Princeton University Press, 1952.

Hernández Aponte, Gerardo Alberto. "'Vuestra Madre' de la Santa Montaña en San Lorenzo, Puerto Rico: ¿La articulación del mito de la Virgen María en la persona de Elena Ache?" *Hispania Sacra* 66, no. 134 (2014): 689–731.

Hernández García, Elizabeth. "'Una columna fortísima del altar y del trono': Pedro Gutiérrez de Cos, Obispo de Huamanga y de Puerto Rico (1750–1833)." *Hispania sacra* 60, no. 122 (July–December 2008): 531–55.

Hernández Hiraldo, Samiri. *Black Puerto Rican Identity and Religious Experience.* Gainesville: University Press of Florida, 2006.

Herzig Shannon, Nancy. *El Iris de Paz: el espiritismo y la mujer en Puerto Rico, 1900–1905.* Río Piedras, PR: Ediciones Huracán, 2001.

Hobsbawm, E.J., and Terence O. Ranger. *The Invention of Tradition.* Cambridge: Cambridge University Press, 1983.

Holland, Clifton L. *Table of Estimated Size of the Protestant Movement in Puerto Rico, 2000.* San Pedro, Costa Rica: PROLADES, 2008.

Igartua, José E. "Quebec and Puerto Rico: Parallel Destinies." *Revista de Ciencias Sociales* 22 (summer 2010): 34–61.

Jiménez Duque, Baldomero. *La espiritualidad en el siglo XIX español.* Madrid: Fundación universitaria española, 1974.

Jones, William Ambrose. *Sínodo diocesano del obispado de Puerto Rico: celebrado en los dias 9, 10 y 11 de enero del año 1917.* San Juan, PR: Tip. Cantero, Fernández & Co., 1917.

Julián de Nieves, Elisa. *The Catholic Church in Colonial Puerto Rico: 1898–1964.* Río Piedras, PR: Editorial Edil, 1982.

Kardec, Allan. *Spiritualist Philosophy: The Spirits's Book, Containing the Principles of Spiritist Doctrine.* Boston, MA: Colby and Rich, 1893.

Keegan, William F. "The 'Classic' Taíno." In *The Oxford Handbook of Caribbean Archaeology,* ed. William F. Keegan, Corinne L. Hofman, and Reniel Rodríguez Ramos, 70–83. New York: Oxford University Press, 2013.

Keegan, William F., and Florida Museum of Natural History. *Taíno Indian Myth and Practice: The Arrival of the Stranger King.* Gainesville: University Press of Florida, 2007.

Klein, Naomi. *The Battle for Paradise: Puerto Rico Takes on the Disaster Capitalists.* Chicago: Haymarket Books, 2018.

Koss, Joan D. "El porqué de los cultos religiosos: el caso del espiritismo en Puerto Rico." *Revista de Ciencias Sociales* 16, no. 1 (1972): 61–72.

– "Religion and Science Divinely Related: A Case History of Spiritism in Puerto Rico." *Caribbean Studies* 16, no. 1 (1976): 22–43.

Laboy Gómez, José Enrique. *Los católicos rebeldes en Puerto Rico durante el período de la guerra fría.* Río Piedras, PR: Publicaciones Gaviota, 2015.

LaRuffa, Anthony L. "Pentecostalism in Puerto Rican Society." In *Perspectives on Pentecostalism: Case Study for the Caribbean and Latin America,* ed. Steven Glazer. Washington, DC: University Press of America, 1980.

– *San Cipriano: Life in a Puerto Rican Community.* New York: Gordon and Breach, 1971.

Linde, Janet R., and Melinda K. Friend. "Victor S. Clark Papers. A Finding Aid to the Collection in the Library of Congress," ed. Library of Congress Manuscript Division. Washington, DC: Library of Congress, 2011.

Loebach, Gregory. "Problems of Religious Practice on the Island." In *Spiritual Care of Puerto Rican Migrants*, ed. William Ferree, Ivan Illich, and Joseph P. Fitzpatrick, part 2, 1–6. New York: Arno Press, 1980.

López Cantos, Ángel. *La religiosidad popular en Puerto Rico, siglo XVIII*. San Juan, PR: Centro de Estudios Avanzados de Puerto Rico y el Caribe, 1993.

López de Haro, Damián. *Constituciones sinodales*. San Juan, PR: Obispo de Puerto Rico, Impr. del seminario, 1920.

– *Sínodo de San Juan de Puerto Rico de 1645. Tierra nueva e cielo nuevo*. Ed. Horacio Santiago-Otero and Antonio Garcia y García. Madrid/Salamanca: Centro de Estudios Históricos del CSIC/Instituto de Historia de la Teología Española de la UPS, 1986.

López Muñoz, Miguel Luis. "La fiesta religiosa en la diócesis de Granada (1750–1825): Opinión, control y represión." *Chronica Nova: Revista de historia moderna de la Universidad de Granada* 21 (1993): 239–78.

López Sierra, Héctor E. "Construcción de identidades afroreligiosa [*sic*] en la modernidad puertorriqueña. El caso de la religión de Ocha e Ifá: Perspectivas fenomenológicas y transdisciplinaria [*sic*]." In *Actualidad de las tradiciones espirituales y culturales africanas en el Caribe y Latinoamérica*, ed. María Elba Torres Muñoz, Marta Moreno Vega, and Mónica Cortés Torres, 201–14. San Juan, PR: Centro de estudios avanzados de Puerto Rico y el Caribe; Instituto de las Tradiciones Afrocaribeñas, 2010.

López Valdés, Rafael L. Email to the author, 21 February 2020.

López Valdés, Rafael L., and Ricardo E. Alegría. *Pardos y morenos esclavos y libres en Cuba y sus instituciones en el Caribe hispano*. San Juan, PR: Centro de Estudios Avanzados de Puerto Rico y el Caribe, 2007.

Loubser, Johannes. "The Ball-court Petroglyph Boulders at Jacaná, South-central Puerto Rico." *Cambridge Archaeological Journal* 20, no. 3 (2010): 323–44.

Macfee, J. Ernest. "To-day in Porto Rico." *Missionary Review of the World* 38 (August 1915): 577–85.

Malavet, Pedro A. *America's Colony: The Political and Cultural Conflict between the United States and Puerto Rico*. New York: New York University Press, 2004.

Manners, Robert A. "Tabara: Subcultures of a Tobacco and Mixed Crops Municipality." In *The People of Puerto Rico*, ed. Julian H. Steward, 93–170. Chicago: University of Illinois Press, 1969.

Mari Mut, José A. *Los pueblos de Puerto Rico y las iglesias de sus plazas*. Puerto Rico: Ediciones Digitales, 2013. http://edicionesdigitales.info/PueblosPR/PueblosPR/Welcome.html.

Martin, David. *Tongues of Fire: The Explosion of Protestantism in Latin America*. Cambridge, MA: Blackwell, 1990.

Martínez, Elena Catalán. "El clero ante la crisis del siglo XVIII. Conflictos y estrategias." *Tiempos Modernos* 7, no. 20 (2010): 1–35.

Martínez-Fernández, Luis. "Crypto-Protestants and Pseudo-Catholics in the Nineteenth-Century Hispanic Caribbean." *Journal of Ecclesiastical History* 51, no. 2 (2000): 347–65.

Martínez Tornero, Carlos A. *Carlos III y los bienes de los jesuítas: la gestión de las temporalidades por la Monarquía borbónica (1767–1815)*. San Vicente del Raspeig, Spain: Publicaciones de la Universidad de Alicante, 2010.

Martín Ramos, Jesús. *Las comunicaciones en la Isla de Puerto Rico, 1850–1898*. San Juan, PR: Academia Puertorriqueña de la Historia, 2006.

Meier, Johannes. "La historia de las diócesis de Santo Domingo, Concepción de la Vega, San Juan de Puerto Rico y Santiago de Cuba desde su inicio hasta la mitad del siglo XVII." In *Historia general de la Iglesia en America Latina. IV – Caribe*, ed. Johannes Meier, 21–151. Salamanca: Ediciones Sigueme, 1995.

Melgarejo, Jhoan. "Memoria y descripción de la isla de Puerto Rico mandata a hacer por S.M. el rey Don Felipe II en el año 1582 y sometida por el ilustre señor Capitán Jhoan Melgarejo, gobernador y justicia mayor en esta ciudad e isla." *Boletín Histórico de Puerto Rico* 1 (1914): 75–91.

Mendelbaum, Diego. Interview by the author with Diego Mendelbaum, spiritual leader of the Shaare Zedek synagogue, San Juan, 6 February 2019.

Mintz, Sidney W. "Cañamelar: The Subculture of a Rural Sugar Plantation Proletariat." In *The People of Puerto Rico*, ed. Julian H. Steward, 314–417. Chicago: University of Illinois Press, 1969.

– "Puerto Rico: An Essay in the Definition of a National Culture." In *Commission on the Status of Puerto Rico. Selected Background Studies*, 339–434. Washington, DC: Government Printing Office, 1966.

– *Worker in the Cane: A Puerto Rican Life History*. New Haven, CT: Yale University Press, 1960.

Mitchell, Mozella G. *Crucial Issues in Caribbean Religions*. New York: Peter Lang, 2006.

Montes Mock, Miriam. "Radio religiosa y la cultura popular en Puerto Rico." MA thesis, Universidad de Puerto Rico, 1991.

Museo de San Juan. *Los Judíos en Puerto Rico/Jews in Puerto Rico*. San Juan, PR: Municipio de San Juan Departamento de Arte y Cultura, 2004.

Negrón de Montilla, Aida. *Americanization in Puerto Rico and the Public-School System 1900–1930*. San Juan, PR: Editorial Universidad de Puerto Rico, 1977.

Ocampo, Tarsicio, ed. *Puerto Rico, Partido Acción Cristiana, 1960–62: documentos y reacciones de prensa*. Cuernavaca, Mexico: Centro Intercultural de Documentación, 1967.

Oliver, José R. *Caciques and Cemí Idols: The Web Spun by Taíno Rulers between Hispaniola and Puerto Rico*. Tuscaloosa: University of Alabama Press, 2009.

– "The Proto-Taíno Monumental *Cemís* of Caguana: A Political-Religious 'Manifesto.'" in *Ancient Borinquen: Archaeology and Ethnohistory of Native Puerto Rico*, ed. Peter E. Siegel, 230–83. Tuscaloosa: University of Alabama Press, 2005.

Ortiz Diaz, Angel Luis. "La manifestación anticlerical en Puerto Rico entre 1870–1900." PhD dissertation, Universidad de Puerto Rico, 1994.

Padilla Seda, Elena. "Nocorá: The Subcultures of Workers on a Government-Owned Sugar Plantation." In *The People of Puerto Rico*, ed. Julian H. Steward, 265–313. Chicago: University of Illinois Press, 1969.

Pané, Ramón, and José Juan Arrom. *An Account of the Antiquities of the Indians*. Durham, NC: Duke University Press, 1999.

Partsch, Jaime. *La crisis de 1898 y su impacto en los institutos de vida religiosa en Puerto Rico*. San Juan, PR: Fundación Puertorriqueña de las Humanidades, 2008.

Patz, Norman R. "In Memory of the Six Million." In *The Book of Memory*, 23–5. San Juan, PR: Temple Beth Shalom of Puerto Rico, 2013.

– Interview by the author with Rabbi Norman Patz, visiting rabbi, Beth Shalom synagogue, Santurce, Puerto Rico, 12 February 2019.

Peña Díaz, Manuel. "Tolerar la costumbre: Ferias y romerías en el siglo XVIII." *Hispania* 74, no. 248 (2014): 777–806.

Perea, Salvador. *Historia de Puerto Rico, 1537–1700*. [San Juan, PR]: Instituto de Cultura Puertorriqueña; Universidad Catolica de Puerto Rico, 1972.

Pérez, Esteban. *Estudio etnográfico de la santería afro-cubana en Puerto Rico*. N.p., 1977.

Pérez Rivera, Jaime Moisés. "La Asociación de Católicos de Ponce (1899–1915): una reacción al proceso de americanización." *Historia y Sociedad* 10 (1998): 49–70.

Picó, Fernando. *Historia general de Puerto Rico*. 4th ed. San Juan, PR: Ediciones Huracán, 2008.

– *Libertad y servidumbre en el Puerto Rico del siglo XIX*. 3rd ed. Río Piedras, PR: Ediciones Huracán, 1983.

– "Rastros rayados: Ponce 1800–1850." Conference, History Department, Universidad de Puerto Rico, Río Piedras, 22 February 2012.

– "La religiosidad popular en el Puerto Rico del siglo 19." In *Vírgenes, Magos y Escapularios*, ed. Ángel G. Quintero Rivera, 151–62. San Juan, PR: Centro de investigaciones sociales, Universidad de Puerto Rico, Río Piedras; Centro de investigaciones académicas, Universidad del Sagrado Corazón; Fundación puertorriqueña de humanidades, 1998.

Pond, Shepard. "The Spanish Dollar: The World's Most Famous Silver Coin." *Bulletin of the Business Historical Society* 15, no. 1 (1941): 12–16.

PROLADES. RITA Database of Puerto Rico, 2017. http://prolades.com/cra/regions/caribe/pri/rita_dbase_prico.htm.

Ramadan-Santiago, Omar. "Introduction of Islam to Sixteenth-Century Puerto Rico." In *Encyclopedia of Latin American Religions*, ed. Henri Gooren, 1–5. Cham, Switzerland: Springer International Publishing, 2016.

Rawlings, Helen. *Church, Religion and Society in Early Modern Spain*. New York: Palgrave, 2002.

Reichard de Cancio, Haydée E. "Desarollo de la religión popular católica en nuestras playas." *Revista Saludos Puertorico.com*, 2012.

– *Puerto Rico: 500 años de la mano de María*. San Juan, PR: Editorial Tiempo Nuevo, 2010.

– *Temas y Temitas*. 2nd ed. Mayagüez, PR, 2006.

Robles Álvarez, Irizelma. *La marejada de los muertos: tradición oral de los pescadores de la costa norte de Puerto Rico*. San Juan, PR: Centro de Investigaciones Sociales, Universidad de Puerto Rico, 2009.

Rodríguez Escudero, Néstor. *Historia del espiritismo en Puerto Rico*. 2nd ed. Quebradilla, PR: Imprenta San Rafael, 1991.

Rodríguez León, Mario A. "Introducción." In *Sínodo de San Juan de Puerto Rico de 1645*, ix–lxii. Madrid/Salamanca: Centro de Estudios Históricos del CSIC/Instituto de Historia de la Teología Española de la UPS, 1986.

Rodríguez Pérez, Lilian del Carmen. "La obra de los Hermanos Cheo (1902–1927)." MA thesis, Centro de Estudios Avanzados de Puerto Rico y el Caribe, 1994.

Rogler, Charles Cordier. *Comerío: A Study of a Puerto Rican Town*. Lawrence: University of Kansas, 1940.

Román, Reinaldo L. *Governing Spirits: Religion, Miracles, and Spectacles in Cuba and Puerto Rico, 1898–1956.* Chapel Hill: University of North Carolina Press, 2007.

– "Spiritists versus Spirit-mongers: Julia Vázquez and the Struggle for Progress in 1920s Puerto Rico." *Centro Journal* 14, no. 2 (2002): 27–47.

Román Vádiz, Alicia. "The Development of the Jewish Community in Puerto Rico during the Years 1940 to 1970." MA thesis, Universidad de Puerto Rico, 1992.

Romero López, Javier. "La reducción de la influencia tradicional católica por el anticlericalismo en Puerto Rico a fines del siglo XIX." MA thesis, Universidad de Puerto Rico, 1989.

Sáez, Florencio. *Entre Cristo y Che Guevara; historia de la subversión política en las iglesias evangélicas de Puerto Rico.* San Juan, PR: Editorial Palma Real, 1972.

Salcedo Chirinos, César Augusto. "Estragos tropicales de la lujuria: las transgreciones venéreas del clero de Puerto Rico, 1798–1852." In *El sexo en la Iglesia,* ed. Samuel Silva Gotay and Luis N. Rivera Pagán, 35–63. Río Piedras, PR: Ediciones Gaviota, 2015.

Sanchez, Angela A. "An Examination of the Folk Healing Practice of Curanderismo in the Hispanic Community." *Journal of Community Health Nursing* 35, no. 3 (2018): 148–61.

Santaella Rivera, Esteban. *Historia de los Hermanos Cheos: Recopilación de escritos y relatos.* Ponce, PR: Editorial Alfa y Omega, 1979.

Santiago Santana, Miguel. *Antulio Parrilla Bonilla: obispo y profeta de Puerto Rico.* San Juan, PR: Fundación El Piloto, 2013.

Sarrailh, Jean. "La crise spirituelle et économique de l'Espagne à la fin du 18e siècle." *Journal of Modern History* 27, no. 1 (1955): 1–13.

Scarano, Francisco A. *Puerto Rico: Cinco siglos de historia.* 3rd ed. San Juan, PR: McGraw-Hill, 2008.

Schroeder, Hannes, et al. "Origins and Genetic Legacies of the Caribbean Taino." *Proceedings of the National Academy of Sciences* (2018): 1–6. http://www.pnas.org/content/pnas/early/2018/02/13/1716839115.full.pdf.

Seda, Eduardo. *Social Change and Personality in a Puerto Rican Agrarian Reform Community.* Evanston, IL: Northwestern University Press, 1973.

Silva Gotay, Samuel. *Catolicismo y política en Puerto Rico bajo España y Estados Unidos: siglos XIX y XX.* San Juan, PR: Editorial Universidad de Puerto Rico, 2005.

– "Desarrollo de la dimensión religiosa del nacionalismo en Puerto Rico 1898–1989." *Estudios interdisciplinarios de America Latina y el Caribe* 1, no. 1 (2015). http://eial.tau.ac.il/index.php/eial/article/view/1311/1337.

– *La iglesia católica de Puerto Rico en el proceso político de americanización: 1898–1930*. Río Piedras, PR: Publicaciones Gaviota, 2012.

– *El pensamiento cristiano revolucionario en América Latina y el Caribe: implicaciones de la teología de la liberación para la sociología de la religión*. Río Piedras, PR: Ediciones Huracán, 1989.

– *Protestantismo y política en Puerto Rico, 1898–1930: hacia una historia del protestantismo evangélico en Puerto Rico*. 2nd ed. San Juan, PR: Editorial de la Universidad de Puerto Rico, 1998.

– "Puerto Rico." In *The Encyclopedia of Caribbean Religions*, ed. Patrick Taylor, Frederick Ivor Case, and Sean Meighoo, 727–9. Champaign: University of Illinois Press, 2013.

– *Soldado católico en guerra de religión: religión y política en España y Puerto Rico durante el siglo XIX*. Río Piedras, PR: Publicaciones Gaviota, 2012.

Silverman, Sydel. "Introduction: The Puerto Rico Project: Reflections Sixty Years Later." *Identities* 18, no. 3 (2011): 179–84.

Stevens Arroyo, Antonio M. "The Catholic Worldview in the Political Philosophy of Pedro Albizu Campos." *US Catholic Historian* 20, no. 4 (2002): 53–73.

– *Cave of the Jagua: The Mythological World of the Taínos*. 2nd ed. Scranton, PA: University of Scranton Press, 2006.

– "The Indigenous Elements in the Popular Religion of Puerto Ricans." PhD dissertation, Fordham University, 1981.

– "The Inter-Atlantic Paradigm: The Failure of Spanish Medieval Colonization of the Canary and Caribbean Islands." *Comparative Studies in Society and History* 35, no. 3 (1993): 515–43.

– "Pious Colonialism: Assessing a Church Paradigm for Chicano Identity." In *Mexican American Religions: Spirituality, Activism, and Culture*, ed. Mario Garcia and Gaston Espinosa, 57–82. Durham, NC: Duke University Press, 2008.

– "Understanding the Work of Diego De Torres y Vargas." In *Report on the Island and Diocese of Puerto Rico (1647) by Canon Diego de Torres y Vargas*, ed. Jaime R. Vidal, 1–22. Scranton, PA: University of Scranton Press, 2010.

Steward, Julian H. *The People of Puerto Rico: A Study in Social Anthropology*. Chicago: University of Illinois Press, 1956.

Sued Badillo, Jalil, and Ángel López Cantos. *Puerto Rico negro*. Río Piedras, PR: Editorial Cultural, 1986.

Torres y Vargas, Diego de, Jaime R. Vidal, and Antonio M. Stevens Arroyo. *Report on the Island & Diocese of Puerto Rico (1647)*. Scranton, PA: University of Scranton Press, 2010.

Tumin, Melvin M., and Arnold S. Feldman. "The Miracle at Sabana Grande." In *Portrait of a Society: Readings on Puerto Rican Sociology*, ed. Eugenio Fernández Méndez. Río Piedras, PR: University of Puerto Rico Press, 1972.

United States. Bureau of the Census. *Fifteenth Census of the United States: 1930. Population*. Vol. 1. Washington, DC: Government Printing Office, 1931.

Uribe, Guillermo. *Les transformations du christianisme en Amérique latine. Des origines à nos jours*. Paris: Karthala, 2009.

Valle Atiles, Francisco del. *El campesino puertorriqueño: sus condiciones físicas[,] intelectuales y morales causas que las determinan y medios para mejorarla. Memoria premiada en el certamen del Ateneo Puertorriqueño*. San Juan, PR: J. Gonzáles Font, 1887.

Valle Ferrer, Norma. *Fiestas de Cruz: tradición y devoción en la comunidad puertorriqueña*. San Juan, PR: Instituto de Cultura Puertorriqueña, 1985.

Vidal, Teodoro. *Oraciones, conjuros y ensalmos en la cultura popular puertorriqueña*. 1st ed. San Juan, PR: Ediciones Alba, 2010.

– *Tradiciones en la brujería puertorriqueña*. San Juan, PR: Ediciones Alba, 1989.

Wagenheim, Olga Jiménez de. *El grito de Lares: sus causas y sus hombres*. 5th ed. San Juan, PR: Ediciones Huracán, 2004.

Wipfler, William. "La Iglesia católica y la dictadura de Trujillo en la República Dominicana." In *Historia general de la Iglesia en America Latina. IV – Caribe*, ed. Johannes Meier, 352–80. Salamanca: Ediciones Sigueme, 1995.

Wolf, Eric R. "San José: Subcultures of a 'Traditional' Coffee Municipality." In *The People of Puerto Rico*, ed. Julian H. Steward, 171–264. Chicago: University of Illinois Press, 1969.

Zaragoza, Edward C. "The Santiago Apóstol of Loíza, Puerto Rico." *Caribbean Studies* 23, no. 1–2 (1990): 125–39.

Zarchi, Rabbi Mendel. Interview by the author with Rabbi Mendel Zarchi, at the Rohr Shabad-Lubovitch synagogue, Isla Verde, 4 March 2019.

Zayas Micheli, Luis O. *Catolicismo popular en Puerto Rico: una explicación sociológica*. Ponce, PR: L.O. Zayas Micheli, 1990.

Index